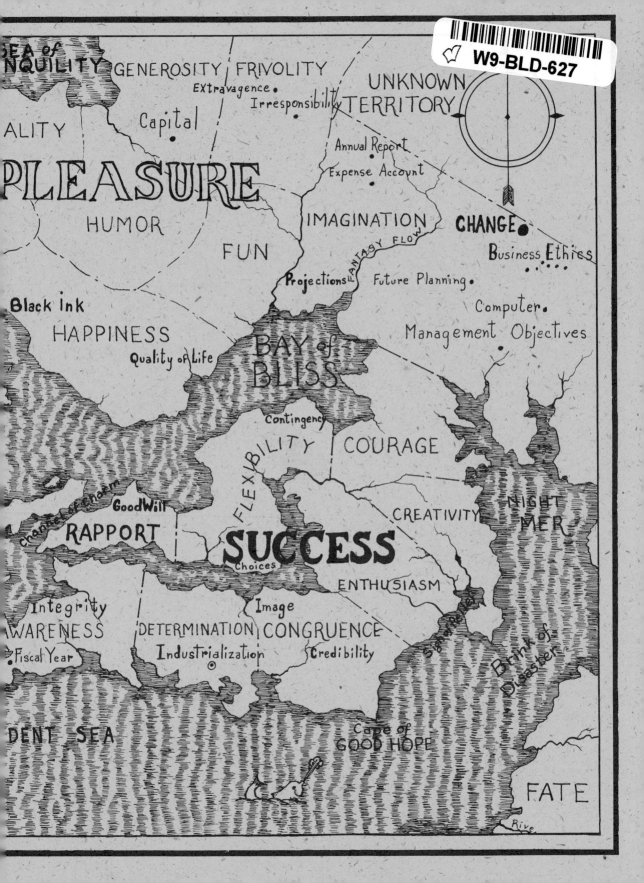

Influencing with Integrity

Management Skills For
Communication and Negotiation

Influencing with Integrity

Management Skills For Communication and Negotiation

Written and Illustrated by
Genie Z. Laborde

SYNTONY PUBLISHING
Palo Alto, California

SYNTONY PUBLISHING

1450 Byron Street
Palo Alto, CA 94301
(415) 324-4450

First clothbound edition published 1984
Syntony paperbound edition published 1987

The Library of Congress has cataloged the first printing of
this title as follows:

Laborde, Genie Z.
    Influencing with integrity: management skills for written communica-
tion and negotiation / written and illustrated by Genie Z. Laborde.
c1983.

    xix, 231 p., A-H p. of plates : ill. (some col), maps ; 25 cm.
    Maps on lining papers.
    Bibliography: p. 207-219
    Includes index.
    ISBN 0-9613172-0-5

    1. Communication in management.   2. Neurolinguistics.   I. Title.
HD30.3.L33   1983   001.51—dc19   83-51129
                                                     AACR 2   MARC

Library of Congress

ISBN 0-9613172-0-5 (hbk)
10-9-8-7
ISBN 0-933347-10-3 (pbk)
10-9-8-7-6-5-4

Printed in the United States of America

This book is dedicated to my husband, George, and my children: Tracy, Cliffe, Gary, Peter, Adrienne, and Kathryn, all of whom have taught me new ways to communicate and negotiate.

Other Syntony Books by Dr. Laborde

*Fine Tune Your Brain: How to Sell Your Idea
to Someone Else*

*90 Days to Communication Excellence:
A Skill-Building Workbook*

Available Fall, 1987:
*Spellbinding: How to Attract and Maintain
a Relationship*

Contents

Foreword   xi

Editor's Note   xiv

Preface   xvi

Acknowledgments   xix

Introduction   1

1   **Outcomes**   7
Aim for a Specific Result   8
Be Positive   11
See/Hear/Feel Sensory Data   11
Dovetail Desires   20
Entertain Short· and
Long·Term Objectives   23

2   **Rapport**   27
Matching Voice Tone or Tempo   30
Matching Breathing   33
Matching Movement Rhythms   34
Matching Body Postures   35

3   **Perception + Thinking**
→ **Communication**   45
Perceptual Doors   51
Representational systems   53
Conscious thought Processes   56
Representational systems and

Eye Movements   58
   Visuals   60
   Auditories   62
   Kinesthetics   64
   Cerebrals   65
The context   67
Matching Representational Systems   68

4   Sensory Acuity   **75**
Unconscious Visible Responses   78
   Skin Color Changes   79
      Photographs   76C, D, E, F
   Minute Muscle Changes   80
      Photographs   76B, G
   Lower Lip Changes   80
      Photographs   76H
   Eye Accessing Cues—Representational System
   Cues
      Photographs   76A
   Rapport   76A
   Breathing Changes   81
Benefits of Sensory Acuity   87

5   The Five Finger Pointers   **89**
Syntonic Learning   91
   Step 1: Recognition   92
   Step 2: Response   94
   Step 3: Recognition—Response   94

Pointer 1: Nouns   92
Pointer 2: Verbs   97
Pointer 3: Rules   98
Pointer 4: Generalizations   101
Pointer 5: Comparators   105

6   Meeting Procedures   **111**
PEGASUS   111
   Present Outcomes   117
   Explain Evidence   117
   Gain Agreement on Outcomes   118
   Activate Sensory Acuity   118
   Summarize Each Major Decision   119
   Use the Relevancy Challenge   120
   Summarize the Next Step   122
How to Take Over a Meeting   124

7   Flexibility   **129**
Meaning is Response/Behavior   131
Uncomplicating Flexibility   132
   Disadvantages of Flexibility   135
   Advantages of Flexibility   136

8   Syntonic Sales Techniques   **141**
Resource State   142
UNICORN   145
   Use Pointers to Clarify Outcomes   145
   Nudge Buyer's See/Hear/Feel Fantasy   146

If, As If, and Future Planning   146
Conditional Close   148
Outcome Dovetailing   150
Rapport   151
Next Step and Summary   151

9   Negotiating with Others   **153**
CHANGE REALITY   158
  Chunk Up/Chunk Down   159
  Hirarchy of Values and
  Hierarchy of Criteria   162
  Another Outcome   171
  Negative Consequences   173
  Generate a Metaphor   173
  Enter a Counter Example   176
  Redefine the Outcome   178
  Effect, Cause and Effect   178
  Apply to Self   179
  Life Equivalents   180
  Intent   180
  Time   181
  Your Map of Reality   182

10   Congruence   **185**

Conclusion   **195**

Glossary   **203**

Bibliography   **207**

Index   **221**

Foreword

Slightly over a decade ago, Richard Bandler and I began the task of creating a set of tools that would serve anyone interested in pursuing and trapping the elusive prey known as human excellence. Much has occurred in the ensuing time. We developed a series of models of human excellence with special emphasis on patterns of communication. We uncovered ways to recognize and codify the specific skills by which excellent communicators achieve their outcomes in fields as disparate as medicine and business.

These models are the result of NLP technology, not NLP itself. The NLP *process* creates the models. In this decade we have taught more than five thousand people to use these models of excellence. Our trainers have probably trained another fifty thousand. From those thousands, I have selected fewer than ten people to work with me as partners. Genie Laborde is one of my partners.

Dr. Laborde is, without a doubt, one of the most skillful, articulate, and successful presenters of the models that have been developed through the NLP process. She employs a powerful and unique set of metaphors in her consulting, her trainings, and here in the book you presently hold. I recognize much of the material she presents here, yet equally, I recognize the special organization and style of expression as being uniquely Genie's.

I cannot, of course, predict the efficacy of her effort for you. I can only confess my interest in and enjoyment of the unique interpretations she offers her readers. I urge you to take her efforts with a sense of adventure, as I did, and to act on the information she presents here.

In a recent interview, two journalists preparing an article for *Science Digest* accused me of being delinquent in policing NLP. I offered them the following metaphor. I am the oldest of nine children and have children of my own. When a man and a woman decide to have a child, they are filled with hopes and dreams of how beautiful, sensitive, and clever their child will be. These dreams provide the parents with a principled way of deciding how to support and promote certain kinds of behavior in their infant, child, and young adult. The wise parent soon discovers the limits of the influence s/he can and should exercise on offspring, and thereby learns to appreciate the unique qualities of the mature human being s/he was instrumental in developing.

Given fifty-five thousand people have been trained, to some degree, I will not police them all. I agree with the journalists that these skills can be used to manipulate. I am delighted that one of my colleagues has undertaken the task of distinguishing manipulation from influencing. I recommend that each of those fifty-five thousand read this book and then pass it to a friend.

John Grinder
Summer 1983

Editor's Note

After reading the original manuscript of this book, I recommended that Science and Behavior decline interest in its publication. The manuscript needed substantial revisions which would strain our resources, and its material and tone struck me as pat, simplistic, and at times incredible.

Two weeks later, I decided to reread it more closely. A number of incidents in the interim had brought to mind so many different passages that I suspected I had misjudged Genie Laborde's work.

Fortunately, the publisher had not. The publication agreement was executed not long after, and I pored over this material word by word. What had seemed pat on first reading was proven out time and again all around me. I experimented with different phrases and tactics, which generally made my life a little easier and a lot more productive. Ultimately, I abandoned the role of grudging skeptic.

Still, this book is too much to absorb in one reading, yet alone one sitting. Don't bother trying. Read it carefully, and then keep it handy. I suspect you (and anyone you influence) will refer to it until and beyond the publication of Genie Laborde's next work.

—R. B.

Preface

If I could teach you everything that is in this book in the first few pages, we could move on—to the next level of communication. That is a rewarding level on which to communicate, and not many people have arrived there. One reason for writing this book was to increase the number of skilled communicators.

If you already knew what is in chapters 3 and 8, then you would understand chapter 1 more thoroughly and more quickly, and you would be more receptive to learning the skills it explains. Understanding and skill rest on each other; as one increases, so does the other. This takes time.

Since words are used sequentially and since we tend to be skeptics when presented with new ways to behave, you may be tempted to dismiss me as just another California flake. But if you can give your skeptic a holiday long enough to test the premises and skills I write about, we can move right along. I'm willing to risk being called a flake on the off chance that these influencing skills will turn up in your repertoire within a short time of your reading about them.

Now for the difference between influence and manipulation. The distinction is simple. Once you know how to clarify your own desires (or *outcomes*, as defined in chapter 1), you can use the same techniques to clarify the outcomes of any other party involved in the communication. Achieving that party's outcome while you achieve your own is what I call influencing with integrity.

Achieving your own outcome at the expense of or even without regard for the other party constitutes manipulation. What makes this particular "informed manipulation" so frightening is that people with these skills acquire such personal power that they are able to affect people deeply, and their capacity to misguide others is thereby increased to the point of evil. I cannot prevent that evil. It exists within those people as a choice they have made. It does not exist within the skills elaborated here.

I recommend influencing over manipulation.

Acknowledgments

Thank you, Bruce Dillman. Without you, this book would not have been completed.

Thank you, Rain Blockley. Without you as editor, this book would be less perfect than it is.

Thank you, John Grinder. You have taught me some useful skills and reminded me of others already learned and forgotten.

Thank you, Brian Van der Horst, for being there when I needed you.

Thank you, Bob Hill, for encouraging me to keep going.

Thank you, Lue McEwan for your commitment to excellence in art production.

Thank you, Vickie Martinez for your extraordinary jacket design.

Thanks to all the participants in my seminars, who invariably teach me something new about communication.

Some people are more skilled at influencing than others.

Introduction

Watching and listening to people who seem to have natural talent for effective communication, experts have concluded that these people's strength is not what they say, but how they say it. Most great communicators have in common certain skills of influence. This book presents some of those skills, which are useful in 95 percent of the communication situations you face.

While the focus here is on business communication, the skills are useful anywhere people interact. The recognition and practice of these skills lead to better choices, better decisions, and even better thinking processes.

In spite of its importance, most of us seldom think about communication. Talking (only one of many ways of communicating) is like breathing. We have done it as long as we can remember, and we certainly do not know how we do it. Sometimes talking is more comfortable than at other times, but basically words come, turn into sentences, and talk just happens. We may suspect sometimes that we could be better at communication, but where to start?

Effective communication begins with the recognition that each of us is unique and different. Sometimes we do not seem to be speaking the same language even when we are using the same words. Good communication skills bridge these differences. Bridging skills are influencing skills: they increase understanding and improve the quality of the goals of each individual in the communication process. Business people in seminars across the United States and throughout Europe are learning these techniques of influence. The result of a merger of psychology and linquistics, this technology was first called psycho-linquistics. From this evolved the Neuro-Linquistic Programming (NLP) model, whose early emphasis was on psychotherapy. Now comes the Syntonic model, a new science designed especially for analyzing and producing excellence in communication. The name derives from the word syntony, which means to be in harmony with self and with others—an appropriate goal for the use of these powerful techniques.

SynTonics

The Syntonic model is concerned with the how (or process) of communication, not the what (or content). Syntonics separates the intricacies of the communication process into discrete steps of easily understood information. Knowing these steps enables you to interact with others successfully.

The first step toward mastery of communication is to know what you want. For many people, this is the most difficult step. Once you know your desired outcome (see chapter 1), you need three skills in order to get it.

- The first skill is sensory acuity. You need to see more and hear more than most people do. This is learnable. You may be surprised at the sensory skills you learn just from using this book.
- The second skill is flexibility. If you are not getting the response you want when you talk, you need to be able to change your behavior until you do.
- The third skill is congruence. All of your subpersonalities—the leader, the follower, the ambitious part, and the goof-off—need to agree on what you want. The alignment of all your different parts will produce congruence in communication.

INCONGRUENCE

RIGID

You already have the skills necessary to begin. Some of you have developed these skills more than others. No matter what level of communication skills you have developed, you will find fine-tuning in these pages. This book is written to help you get what you want by using your innate skills consciously as well as unconsciously.

Sensory acuity

Effective communication is like taking a trip. First, you decide on your destination. Then you consider how to go and whom to invite to go with you. You could fly, drive, bicycle, or walk. Say you decide to drive. You then need to find the route that most appeals to you. While proceeding, you need to remember or see checkpoints and landmarks that indicate whether you are on the right road. If your fellow travelers have a destination other than yours, you need to find out at what point they want to proceed on their own. Then, once you arrive at your destination, you need to have specific ways to know this is indeed where you want to be and that you have accomplished everything you wanted.

So, just as travel begins with setting a destination, effective communication begins its process with the recognition of a desired result. In syntonics, we call this an outcome.

FℓeXibiLiTy

Congruence

1
Outcomes

Communicating without a desired outcome is like traveling without a destination. You may end up in a place you really enjoy, or you may not. Enjoying your trip is a perfectly good outcome; ending up at the destination you want is also productive.

An *outcome* is the result you want, defined in terms of the way you would like to *see* things happen, the way you want to *feel*, and what you will *hear* when you have your outcome.

Most business people already know about goal-setting and management by objective. You may have placed the word outcome in the same category. But goals and objectives are in a broader category than outcomes. Outcomes are goals that have been clarified and finely honed by the use of the following five steps. In other words, if goals and objectives are like new pencils just out of a box, outcomes are like sharpened pencils that are ready to do what you want. And the following five steps are the pencil-sharpener.

A. Aim for a specific result
B. Be positive
C. See/hear/feel sensory data
D. Dovetail your desires with those of your communication partner
E. Entertain short- and long-term objectives

These are known as the ABCs of outcomes. Once you understand and implement these steps, you will be able to determine your outcome. Also, you will have an alphabetic mnemonic device.

AIM FOR A SPECIFIC RESULT

Specifying an outcome or a series of outcomes is the first step. Being specific entails expressing your outcome in sensory-based terms: the sights, sounds, and feelings you want to experience. Simultaneously, your attention focuses on external and internal resources that can help you achieve this outcome.

Specifying an outcome can immediately change what you see, hear, and feel. Since you cannot be consciously aware of everything around you, you select certain things and pay attention to them. To a large extent, your outcome of the moment determines which external and internal stimuli you select as worthy of your attention.

Try this exercise: Look at all the colors in the area around you. Name five colors you see. Next, listen to the sounds. Name three. Now notice how your stomach feels. Name the feeling in your stomach.

In doing this, you are in control of your selection process. A conscious outcome sets up the same kind of controlled selection process. This selection, in turn, has a significant impact on your thinking process: what you think about are the pictures, words, or feelings you have selected. You will notice what is available in your immediate environment and among past experiences to assist you. You may select perceptions from your external or internal worlds, from your present or your past experiences, but you cannot think in a vacuum. Your thoughts will be intimately connected to your perceptions. And if you have had experiences that may help you attain your conscious outcome, you can put them to work as a resource.

WE
select
wHAT
WE

SEE
HEAR
feel

We select what we see hear and feel from amidst the booming confusion around us

These perception/thinking processes are complex. If we slow down the perception and thinking processes, we find:

- We notice what is useful for our outcome.
- We remember what is useful for our outcome.
- Our outcome determines our selection of perceptions.
- Our outcome affects our thought processes.
- Our thoughts and perceptions can help us gain our outcome.

Unlike outcomes, goals can be quite nonspecific. Executives and accountants nod their heads when they hear the goals "increased productivity" and "bottom-line results," for example. Neither of these terms is specific enough to be an outcome, though. "A $400,000 increase over last fiscal year's sales without retooling or personnel increase" is more precise, but it is still not an outcome. Being specific is simply the first step.

We notice what is useful for our outcome

We remember what is useful for our outcome from past learnings

For now, all you need to know is: Our outcomes determine perceptual selection

BE POSITIVE AND
SEE/HEAR/FEEL SENSORY DATA

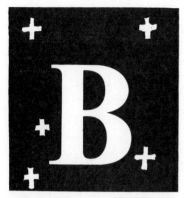

These two steps must be considered together, for they are as intertwined as the cortical neurons of the brain. In fact, they help us get what we want by utilizing the ways our brains process information.

Seemingly simple, these steps are actually important breakthroughs in the study of communication: the results of the intricate postulates of Alfred Korzybski and Noam Chomsky concerning language and brain processing, and the psycho-linguistic insights of Fritz Perls, Milton H. Erickson, Richard Bandler, and John Grinder.

It is important to understand, first, that outcomes are based on sensory experience. This means that an outcome is stated in words that describe what you see and hear and how you feel. (For the purpose of this book, scents and tastes are usually considered part of the *kinesthetic*, or feeling, class of experience.)

By definition, these see/hear/feel descriptions are positive in that they describe what you want to experience rather than what you do not want. "Not to be poor" is negative, for example, while "to be rich" is positive.

Once you can state your outcome in a positive way, then ask yourself, "What will I see when I attain my outcome? What will I hear? What will I feel?" If we continue the outcome of being rich, one set of answers could be:

SEE	HEAR	FEEL
$100,000 in crisp green bills	Crackle of bills	Excitement
Swimming pool	Congratulations by friends	Champagne bubbles
New car	Music by Mozart	Walking on air
Name in lights	Shouts and cheers	Impulse to smile

"Rich" is a word with many meanings. Eliza Doolittle wanted a room somewhere and an easy chair. It would take millions of dollars to make some of us feel rich, but

Eliza wanted an easy chair. If you know what rich means to you, you can learn what is important to you and begin to focus your attention and behavior in ways to gain your outcome. If it takes money, then you can focus on getting money. You may be surprised to find that you do not need money to get the feelings, things, or sounds you want; you may only need better communication skills.

To that end, you need to know the difference between fat, abstract words and lean, concrete words. *Abstract* words are nonspecific. When people describe "rich" in see/hear/feel terms, for example, their answers vary widely. Freedom, productivity, and happiness are other fat, low-quality words. Fat words are favorites of politicians, because these words are so general that the audience can agree with whatever the politician says. With abstract words, each listener can color in his own meaning. Fat words are useful, then, when the speaker is trying to gain agreement among many people.

Concrete words are much more specific. "Bananas" describes a specific fruit. Your bananas may be green and my bananas may be yellow, but we will pretty well agree what "bananas" refers to. The overlap of your meaning and my meaning makes "bananas" a *lean* word.

Fat words have many layers of meanings, while lean words have been pared down to essentials. Fat words are used to gain agreement, lean words, to get insights and give instructions. When your outcome includes tasks or decisions, you need lean words. To discover your own personal outcomes, you need lean, concrete words. This is the purpose of sensory based data: to peel away the fat—the superfluous meanings—until you get to the core of what this outcome means to you.

Fat words are favorites of politicians.

For tasks or decisions, use lean words.

Is a fat, abstract word

Is a lean, concrete word

We
select
what
we
see
hear
&
feel

We tend to remember what is useful for our outcome from past experiences

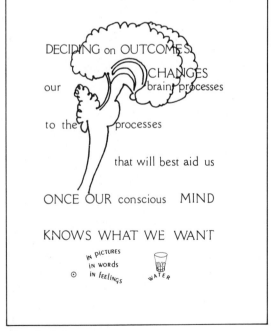

Perceptual selection is determined by our outcome

The following account shows how this information is useful when combined with the ABCs of outcomes. You may find the story too simplistic, unbelievable, or even magical. But it did happen this way. (Note: Some of the terms in the margin have not been explained yet. They will be.)

Processes of Communication

I was a consultant at a computer manufacturing company when the chief executive officer (CEO) asked me to talk to one of his engineers. The engineer in question seemed confused about his work objectives. "He's a good man," the CEO said, "But too hard on himself."

In a corner office, I was met by a tall man whose shoulders hunched forward. He had a concave chest and a mouth with downturned corners. He introduced himself, "I'm Jim Banks," and motioned to a chair. He pulled up his own chair and sat facing me in front of his desk. He was well-dressed but dejected.

As I looked around his large office, all the bright colors I had seen throughout the complex seemed to have drained away. Had the sun gone behind a cloud?

Jim began talking immediately, requesting that I teach him how to get out of his own way. I asked for clarification, not being sure what he meant by the phrase, "get out of my own way."

The individual's meaning of words

"I want to stop sabotaging myself." He looked out the large windows without seeming to see the spring garden, the oak tree, the blue sky.

"OK," I replied, "And when you do stop sabotaging yourself, what will you have?"

"I'll stop being frustrated, angry, and upset."

"I understand that you now feel frustrated, angry, upset. What would you like to feel instead?" The flowers in the garden were still glowing with color. The gray miasma was only in this office.

A long, uncomfortable silence ensued. Uncomfortable for him, not me. I was fascinated that he had ready access to so many negative goals and no positive ones. How could this be? He had the introspective look of one who spent lots of time alone, searching for meaning, and yet. . .

"I don't seem to know what I want." He was right. "I have lots of anxiety about the way I waste time, the way I begin projects and peter out. I don't seem to be able to complete anything. Not at work. Not at home. I start off great. Then I bog down. My boss is irritated. My girl friend is thinking of moving out. I want to be able to complete something."

Aim for a specific outcome

"Great. And now, what specifically would you like to complete?"

"Oh, any one of ten different projects I'm in the middle of."

"Would you be willing to tell me about one?"

Incongruence in voice tone and tempo

"Oh, OK. There's one project," he nodded toward a cabinet, "that I could finish with a little more research. Yes, it's close to finished. Four hours." His voice trailed off.

"Do you really want to finish that project?"

"No."

Be positive

"What would you like to complete?" The soft spring sunlight felt heavy. My shoulders were beginning to hunch like his. I straightened slightly.

"I hate finishing projects, because then I know I haven't done my best work, and once the project is done, I'll never be able to add more to it."

Be positive

"I hear what you hate. What would you like? Before you answer, would you take a deep breath?"

Breathing

He looked surprised, but did take a breath, then said, "I'd like to feel better about my work."

Resource state

"Have you ever felt satisfied with a project you've completed?"

"Not in a long time. Not since I was maybe seventeen or eighteen. I'm thirty-eight. That's a long time to feel frustrated at your own mediocre performance."

A resource state is your optimum emotional and physical condition, in which the resources you have gathered during your life are readily available to you.

"Sure is."

We sat there for a while in silence.

"Would you like to feel satisfied with your own competence?" I asked.

"How could I do that? If I don't feel competent, I'm not competent. I don't want to feel something that's not true."

"I've been here," I looked at my watch, "for some

time, and I've yet to find out your outcome. What do you want?"

Be positive

He was getting irritated.

"I told you I want to stop feeling anxious and frustrated all the time."

"And if you were not feeling anxious and frustrated, what would you like to feel?"

Be positive

Another long silence.

I finally asked, "Satisfied?"

He tried that out, then gave a tiny nod and said, "Yes, satisfied. I don't have to be extraordinarily competent. Just satisfied with my ability."

Straightening my shoulders again, I took a deep breath. At last, we had an outcome, not a goal. Outcomes are stated in positive terms. Outcomes are specific. Outcomes are stated in see/feel/hear terms. Jim would have to remember one of the real outcomes he had achieved earlier and how the experience had looked, sounded, and felt.

Breathing

"OK. Now we can go somewhere. Have you ever felt satisfied with your ability?"

Feel? (As in see/hear/feel)

He looked much younger and a little sheepish as he asked, "Does it matter how long ago?"

"No."

"OK. When I was seventeen, I won an award for a project I did." The change in his physiology was so swift that I blinked, trying to catch the shift.

"Terrific. Can you remember that feeling of satisfaction and maybe even amplify it so that you can really notice how it felt?" His face relaxed, his nose seemed to soften, rosy color came into his face, and a different computer expert sat in front of me. One who was satisfied with one project, twenty years ago.

"What were you looking at when you realized you were satisfied with your own work?" I asked.

See?

"I was looking at the award. I was in my room alone just looking. It was a plaque. I'd placed it on my dresser; it leaned against the wall."

"What did you hear?"

Hear?

"I heard myself saying, 'That was a pretty good project.'" As he said these words, a trace of the old "satisfied" expression crossed his face.

"Could you tell yourself that now?"

"What?"

Resource state

"Would you be willing to say to yourself, 'That was a pretty good project'?" As I completed the question, I could see he had just completed doing what I suggested. The "satisfied" expression crossed his face again.

His voice sounded gruff as he said, "That's silly. That was twenty years ago."

"Silly, yes, maybe. On the other hand, how do you feel now?"

A pause.

"I feel great. . .but will it last?"

**Resource state
See/hear**

"I don't know, but you sure look better. I'm wondering— if you need to—would you be willing to see that plaque once more on your dresser in your mind's eye and say to yourself once more, 'That's a pretty good project'?"

"That's all I have to do to feel satisfied? That seems kind of dumb to me."

"Not nearly as dumb as going around feeling frustrated, anxious, and down on yourself for twenty years."

Hear

He laughed. "You're right." A pause while he tried the phrase again. I could see his face change as he said to himself, "That's a pretty good project." His voice was incredulous. "It works. Why does it work?"

"Well, I know some of the reasons, but not all of them. Our brains are interconnections of neurons and dendrites which work through chemical reactions. Thoughts activate certain chemicals. You just activated a set of satisfaction thought-patterns made by chemicals that your brain knew about, but you haven't used them in a long time."

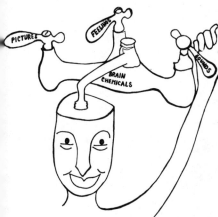

Chemicals in the brain can create a resource state which is based on a past experience. To learn how to generate those chemicals, see Chapter 8.

"Will I be able to finish projects now?" His voice sounded seventeen, and he changed it on the "now" to a lower tone.

"I don't know. Can you imagine yourself spending four hours to complete the project you talked about earlier?"

"It would only take two. . . . Yes." His voice sounded full and decisive. A month later, Jim had completed all his current projects and was busy with a set of new ones.

Resource state

OUTCOMES

To summarize what we have learned about outcomes: An outcome must be stated in positive terms. To "stop doing X" is more of a goal than an outcome. Goals are difficult. Outcomes are easy. Going for what you do not want is a booby trap. Going for what you want is an outcome. Decide what you do want, then ask yourself:

- What will I see when I get my outcome?
- What will I hear?
- What will I feel?

Write down your answers. Try to imagine four things you will see when you have your outcome, then four sounds you will hear, then four sensations you will feel. If you do not know at least four answers in each category, write down as many as you can find.

The procedures in this book will help you specify your outcome in any situation, recall as many resources as you need, and achieve your outcome in a way that may surprise you. This happened to Marianne, who came to me with the goal of winning her sex discrimination lawsuit and ended up with the outcome of a job that paid double money and triple satisfaction over her previous job.

Marianne's attorney had suggested she see me before instigating a sex-discrimination lawsuit against her brokerage firm. She probably had sufficient grounds for a lawsuit, but the attorney thought she would be better served by finding another solution to her situation. The attorney said Marianne's goal was to learn how to like her job.

When Marianne arrived at my office, she was walking slowly, with her head lowered and her eyes looking down and to the right. As she began telling me how much she hated her job and how her boss talked down to her as if she were stupid, her eyes filled with tears. She said her next goal was to stop feeling unappreciated and put down. She was underpaid and employed in a job for

Where is your communication headed?

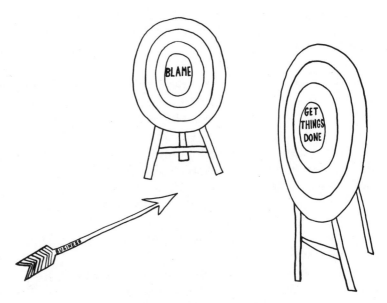

which she was extremely overeducated.

I asked, "What do you want to feel instead of unappreciated and put down?"

She immediately lightened, sat up straight, rubbed her tears away with the back of her hand, and put her feet firmly on the floor. She took a breath, looked thoughtful, then replied, "I have an MBA. I want to feel competent and responsible, like a valued employee who can handle problems that need creative solutions."

If I had been her boss at that moment, I would have been willing to turn any important problem over to her. Ten minutes before, her resentment, disappointment, and dissatisfaction would have alienated me. She was caught in a feedback loop with her boss: her resentment triggered his concern for her competence. He thought he could not trust her, so he gave her less and less responsibility, which merely increased her resentment.

Once Marianne declared her positive intent, she decided to resign her job, drop her idea of a lawsuit, and find a job that fit her qualifications. She accomplished all this within a month. She simply needed to discover her true outcome.

DOVETAIL DESIRES

For the present, entertain the notion that the only way to get your outcome is to see that everyone else involved gets his or her outcome, too. This may sound more difficult than it actually is. Once you are familiar with the see/feel/hear questions, you can find out another's outcome in a few minutes. Say, for instance, that your assistant came in to say she did not feel satisfied with her job.

- Your first question could be, "What would you see if you were satisfied?"
- Your next question could be, "What would you hear if you were satisfied?"
- If necessary, your last question could be, "How would you feel if you were satisfied?"

In the short run, you can stomp on people. In the long run, you pay and pay.

With the information from these questions you can, perhaps, adapt the job to fit her criteria or adapt her criteria to fit the job. Or help her find another job. Once you know her outcome, you can step back and allow yourself to figure out how to get yours and hers at the same time. This is called *matching* or *dovetailing* outcomes.

Dovetailing outcomes ensures your own personal integrity and shows respect for the other person's integrity. While you cannot set other people's outcomes, you can often aid them in attaining what they want. Dovetailing outcomes is the intelligent way to insure your own outcomes, because the others involved become your allies, not your saboteurs. Most people will help you attain your outcome if they can also gain their own in the process.

Manipulation, on the other hand, is talking or acting without regard for others' outcomes. Marie Antoinette paid a high price for this kind of behavior. If you disregard your colleagues' outcomes, they may not use a guillotine, but they will sabotage you covertly, overtly, or both.

One of my first clients was a famous businessman

Manipulation is the opposite of dovetailing.

The Four Rs

RESENTMENT, RECRIMINATION, REMORSE, and REVENGE. The four dragons who lie in wait for those who manipulate. Tom Loarie of American Heyer-Schulte gave a good example of this in a speech after he learned about dovetailing. His concluding sentence was, "Those executives who rise by undercutting others are visible for a short time, then they disappear from the corporate scene."

who bulldozed his way through the corporate world. Winning was his creed and the subtleties of rapport and dovetailing were not for him. He once told me a personal anecdote, hoping I would shed some light on an event that made no sense to him. A few months before, the best secretary he had ever had had suddenly resigned. To try to convince her to stay, he took her to lunch and was warming up to his "I really need you" pitch. She suddenly leaned forward and announced, "I've hated every day I've worked for you and today is the happiest day of my life." With that, she stood up and walked out.

For years, I was not aware of the penalty one pays when outcomes are not dovetailed. When anyone took advantage of me and went for his or her outcome without considering mine, I resented it and wanted to get even. Usually, I settled for resentment and then forgot the incident. I also avoided interacting with that person from then on.

Later, I realized I could often even the score by speaking my true assessment of a situation or a person. More often, the same thought processes that led someone to treat me unfairly created opportunities for a third party to remedy the injustice. Revenge has never been one of my favorite pastimes, but I cannot help but notice when people are served their just desserts.

Just desserts are inevitably served when you are true to yourself.

People sometimes find it difficult to dovetail outcomes. In some cases, you have another choice: go your separate ways. If this is not an option, then you have to spend time and energy searching for ways to satisfy both outcomes. As soon as you realize that your respective outcomes seem to conflict, be sure that both of you have described them in sensory-based words. This step often helps people find creative routes to achieve both sets of desires.

Difficult dovetailing, which involves other communication skills, is described in detail in chapter 9.

ENTERTAINING LONG- AND SHORT-TERM OBJECTIVES

What do you want now?
What do you want ten (or twenty) years from now?

These questions are examples of how to figure out your own short-term and long-term outcomes. Unless you know your outcomes, your attention is random and unfocused. Thinking follows old mental programs, which in turn determine behavior. Perceptions based on an outcome, on the other hand, can immediately focus and improve the whole process of thinking and behavior.

Long- and short-term outcomes sometimes appear to conflict. On April 15, many of us would prefer to take it easy rather than complete those tax forms that have to be postmarked by midnight. When taking it easy conflicts with saving the money of a late fee, we have a choice. Our choices from moment to moment decide our future.

Many of us set up outcomes that are less than we could attain. We then overshoot our short-term outcomes, achieving more than we had thought possible. If we know where we want to go, though, we will overshoot our outcomes in the right direction. I once went

to a corporate training department to discuss presenting a three-day communication seminar. It turned out
that they wanted a twenty-day program. I created a
twenty-day seminar, which also satisfied one of my long-
term outcomes.

When you find yourself overshooting with some regu-
larity, set your long-term outcomes very high and see
how far along that trajectory you can travel with your
short-term outcomes.

At this point, you may be feeling concerned about being too goal-oriented and too focused and aggressive in
your behavior. I applaud your concern. Extreme single-
mindedness can be acceptable behavior in some corporate cultures, but it is inappropriate, even objectionable,
in most.

One safeguard is to have a wide range of outcomes,
choosing those that are appropriate to each situation as
it arises. Another safeguard is to maintain normal sensory acuity and to notice feedback from others so that
you can recognize when you are behaving in an objectionable way. (The exercises in chapter 4 will increase
your sensory acuity and your ability to read feedback.)
The sensitive use of feedback from other people is essential in gaining outcomes. So is the establishment of
rapport, which leads us to the next chapter.

*The most important concept
in this chapter: Dovetailing
outcomes doubles your
chances of winning.*

Drawing by Saxon;
c 1968
The New Yorker
Magazine, Inc.

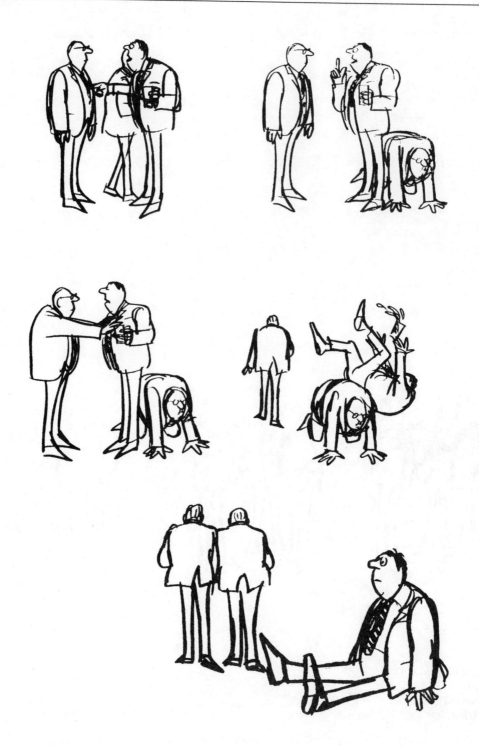

2
Rapport

Rapport is a somewhat exotic English word derived from the French verb *rapporter*, meaning to bring back or refer. The English meaning—a relation of harmony, conformity, accord, or affinity—indicates the importance of rapport to communication. It is the most important process in any interaction. (You thought rapport was a state, right? No. It is a process.)

Without rapport, you will not get what you want—not money, not promotions, not friends. You may not even be able to get a letter typed correctly, unless you do it yourself. Rapport is like money: it increases in importance when you do not have it, and when you do have it, a lot of opportunities appear.

How do you know when you have rapport? Different people have different ways of ascertaining rapport. Personally, I know that I have it by a certain level of comfort—a sense of shared understanding. You may have another way to sense it.

If rapport is present, proceed toward your outcome. If it is missing, then you can be assured neither of you will gain your outcome until rapport is present.

How can you create rapport? Actually, you have done it many times. Establishing rapport seems to be a natural tendency among most people when they get together. When it is not, you can use certain skills to create rapport consciously.

First, check your trust in the competence of the other person to complete the task at hand. In the preceding chapter, for example, a lack of confidence began the cycle of dissatisfaction between Marianne and her boss. He was not necessarily a male chauvinist. He simply did not trust Marianne's competence. Her resentment reinforced his distrust. The cycle escalated with each interaction. If either one had known how to establish rapport, the ending could have been quite different.

Suppose your secretary has retyped the same letter three times and has made typos each time. Now what? You need, at this point, to find out the typist's outcome. Is s/he trying to create a business letter? Is s/he trying to drive you crazy? Is s/he always producing typos? Does s/he have a polarity response (i.e., knowing what you want and doing the opposite)? Do you need an automatic eraser on the typewriter, or do you need a new employee whose outcome dovetails with yours?

You can ask such questions belligerently or simply to find out more information. The greatest part of establishing rapport is often accomplished nonverbally. (Techniques are explained below.) If you are empathetic or *sympatico*, you may turn up information that you can use for establishing trust, and rapport may follow. You may discover, say, that the typist's boyfriend moved out last night, and her outcome is to survive the day so she can cry herself to sleep. Her keys may be sticking together and her typewriter needs overhauling. Or she may be looking for another job and wants to get fired so she can look full time.

When rapport is not present, it becomes top priority in communication.

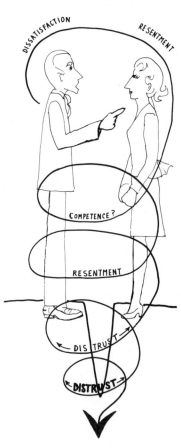

Human beings and their moment-to-moment out-comes are a constant source of surprise or disaster, depending on your point of view. By finding out her outcome for the next thirty minutes and giving her your outcome, you may get a matching set of outcomes. By focusing on outcomes instead of problems, you may also achieve trust, rapport, and a few correct paragraphs.

Liking the other party is not a prerequisite for rapport. Mutual confidence in competence for the task at hand is. If credibility cannot be established, consider changing the task.

Rapport rests on mutual trust in competence for the task at hand.

This book deals with 95 percent of the situations you will face. For that 95 percent, you can establish rapport in many ways. In fact, there are as many different ways to establish rapport as there are individuals. Most of us already have many ways that work most of the time. But there are times when these intuitive ways do not work. What can you do then?

A process called *mirroring* works extraordinarily well to gain rapport if mutual trust in competence is already established. Mirroring is the matching of certain behaviors of the other person. The four mirroring techniques are: matching voice tone or tempo or both; matching breathing; matching rhythms of movements with a different movement; and matching body postures.

These mirroring events often occur naturally as a result of rapport. Mirroring can also be used to establish and increase rapport. However, these techniques may not work unless both or all parties have already established trust in each other's competence.

MATCHING VOICE TONE OR TEMPO

Matching the other person's voice tone or tempo is the best way to establish rapport in the business world.

Some voices coo.   *Some voices gravel at you.*

Tones are high or low, loud or soft. Tempos are fast or slow, with pauses or without pauses. Most people are completely unaware of their own vocal tones or tempos, and they will not notice that you are matching them. Also, voice matching does not have to be exact, just close enough to encourage the other person to feel understood. Usually overlooked, this is the obvious way to establish rapport over the telephone.

One manager acknowledged this information with the statement, "So that's why our department reports so many disgruntled responses from customers in the deep South. We thought Southerners were just difficult to deal with. The personnel in my department phone our customers all over the States to remind them to send in their payments. Our telephone personnel are from New York City. Southerners speak at vastly different rates from New Yorkers. Our policy is to be courteous, but we need to do more than that."

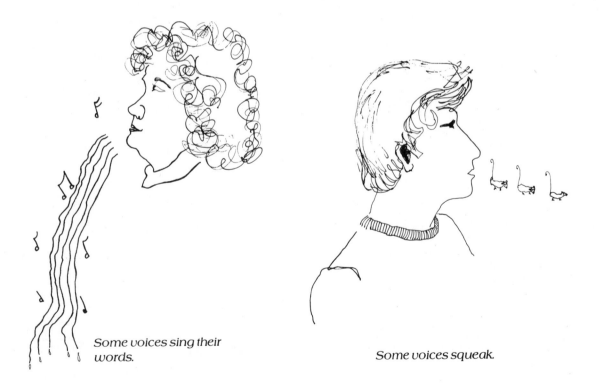

Some voices sing their words.

Some voices squeak.

Another executive received an insurance settlement shortly after he learned about matching tempo. His car had been stolen during the night from in front of his apartment on Staten Island. After weeks of negotiation and nonpayment by the insurance company, he phoned their head office in Dallas, Texas. He was immediately aware that the woman on the other end of the line had a very different tone and tempo from his. His lifelong love of music gave him a discriminating ear, and he was able to match her tempo, even though his tone was a great deal lower. According to him, not only did he get a larger cash settlement than he had expected but his check was mailed the very next day.

Match voice tempo and tone unless several people are together. In that case, don't.

Ways to rapport

A word of caution is needed here. If your tempo is extremely different from that of the other person, go easy on your voice adjustment. If you are a native New Yorker and you suddenly shift to a Southern drawl, you may be in trouble. Instead of a sudden dramatic change, make a small move in the direction of the other's tempo. Slowing your tempo down slightly is not likely to be noticed.

In fact, none of the techniques you learn here for developing rapport should ever be noticed. Be elegant in using these skills: use the least number of moves necessary to solve your problem. A slight adjustment in tempo is probably all you need if you know what you want and are focused on determining another's real outcome. Being truly interested in what the other person wants in an interaction is the most powerful way to produce rapport.

Matching tempo can be learned. The first step is to become aware of different rates of speech, then practice matching in a safe environment. Later, matching tones will increase your ability to establish rapport.

MATCHING BREATHING

The second way to establish rapport is to match the other person's breathing rate. Most people's breathing rate can be perceived easily with a little practice. However, if the person is wearing several layers of clothing, such as a shirt, vest, and jacket, you may have difficulty picking up the movement in his chest or abdomen. Some people have shallow breathing with little outside movement. In these more difficult cases, the edge of the person's shoulder silhouetted against any background will usually show a discernible rise and fall.

One thing you can count on: the other person is breathing. If they have been unsuccessful in the business world for a long time, s/he may be barely breathing, but if you persist in watching, you *can* find the breathing rhythm. Once you have this rhythm, you can pace yourself to it. You may need practice, but this will not take long to learn.

MATCHING MOVEMENT RHYTHMS

Matching movement rhythms, or *crossover mirroring* is a more complex matching. Identify some movement that the other person displays repeatedly and match it with a different movement of your own. For example, each time the other person scratches his chin, you might tap a pencil on the desk.

One of our students used crossover mirroring for the first time on one of her firm's senior vice-presidents (something I would not recommend). Just after our three-day seminar, Trudy faced a meeting for budget approval of a project she wanted very much. The problem was that the vice-president who had to give budget approval was known to be very cool on this type of project. She phoned my partner in New York and said she knew she needed rapport but could think of no way to establish it with this man. He was nervous and full of energy, whereas she is relaxed and has naturally slow movements. They were a complete mismatch.

My partner reminded her of crossover mirroring. During the subsequent meeting, she minimally tapped her foot as he paced up and down. On each of his turns, she changed the foot tapping. It worked. She established rapport and proceeded to get her project approved.

"But maybe it wasn't the crossover mirroring," say the skeptics. Maybe it was her warm personality. Maybe it was the negative ions in the air that day. Each of us has a unique map of reality, and the name of any given locale varies from map to map, just as explanations of or rationales behind a given behavior vary from person to person. Syntonic techniques are significant not necessarily *per se*, but because using them with integrity seems to correspond with attaining one's outcome. And Trudy got her outcome.

Crossover mirroring is almost never noticed, because most of us are unaware of our habitual movements, such as pushing back our eyeglasses, patting our hair, or rubbing our noses. If the other person repeats movements such as these, you can match his or her rhythm

Matching rhythms may seem a far-fetched way to set up rapport. Do not take my word for this — go out and try it.

Say you are in an interaction and notice a lack of harmony, use rapport.

by tapping a pencil, jiggling a foot, or drumming your finger. Once you create rapport, you can move on toward your outcome.

> Why does matching build rapport? Good question. We are not sure we have all the answers. Rapport seems to be similar to rhythm entrainment, a natural phenomenon described by Itzhak Bentov in *Stalking the Wild Pendulum.* Different sized clocks with the same sized pendulums, when placed together on a wall, will gradually synchronize their swings. Discussing this phenomenon in machines and in man, Bentov concludes, "Nature finds it more economical in terms of energy to have periodic events that are close enough in frequency to occur in phase or in step with each other."

MATCHING BODY POSTURES

The last matching technique is the easiest but also the most obvious: simple mirroring of body postures.

"Mimicry?" you may ask. "Is that really a good idea, to mimic someone else's movement?"

Only if you want to establish rapport and do not already have it. There is a fine line between mimicry and emulation. Lean toward emulation and you will do fine.

Matching postures must be done with subtlety, if at all. Otherwise, it is embarrassing to you and irritating to oth-

ers. People may think you are making fun of them. While simple mirroring may occur spontaneously in rapport situations, it can be a booby trap for the novice.

If you decide to check out simple mirroring for yourself, do so in a no-risk situation. Do not test it on your supervisors. It can be great fun on a bus or a plane, though. Do not be surprised if strangers begin talking to you in a friendly way. Another test of this premise is to watch people mirror each other unknowingly in restaurants, airports, and other places. You may be surprised *not* to have noticed natural mirroring occurring all around you.

Rapport during severance minimizes lawsuits.

side by side
RAPPORT

Maintaining rapport is a way to synchronize the different experiences, values, and meanings of human beings. External matching accentuates similarities and plays down differences so that understanding and rapport between the people seem to increase.

You may feel it is unfair to utilize a natural phenomenon such as this to gain an outcome. Remember, though, that you will not gain and retain your own outcome unless you keep the other's outcome in mind. Rapport thus becomes a tool for both of you.

To review the rapport skills: first, check out whether you have it. If so, proceed with your outcome. If not, check out your own trust in the other person's competence for the task at hand. If you trust the person, proceed. If not, find a way to establish trust or to suspend judgment.

Another possible obstacle is that the other person does not trust you. This is where establishing rapport becomes interesting. Rapport is not mechanical. Nor is it as simple as it seems to those of us who have always set it up intuitively. If you gather that the other person does not trust you, you need to find a way to establish personal credibility for the task at hand, or change the task at hand to one for which you can gain credibility. You can always say, "You look busy. I'll come back another day," and trust the person's competence to show you the door. Use the interim time to improve your credibility with letters of recommendation, well-written brochures, or phone calls from satisfied customers. You may need to be creative in establishing your competence if the other person is in doubt.

You can even be direct and say something such as, "You seem to have doubts about my ability to produce results. What, specifically, would you like to see (or hear) that would convince you I can do exactly what I promise?" The skeptic may be willing to give you criteria, and you will know whether you can meet those requirements. If not, a handshake and a goodbye are in order.

There are times when rapport can be and even should be deliberately broken. How do you do this? Look at your watch. This almost always works. Increase your distance from the other person until you are too far away for easy hearing. Or make an abrupt, unexpected movement.

Why would you want to break rapport? To breathe at your own rate, for one. When I first learned of rapport and how it worked, I realized why I was often short of breath. I naturally breathe deep in my abdomen and slowly. When I was in rapport with upper-chest fast breathers, I was uncomfortable. And I seemed to be in rapport with everyone automatically, without knowing it. The week I recognized this, I went around breaking rapport right and left.

Another time to break rapport is when you are about to sign a binding contract. Some levels of rapport set up such a cooperative pull that you may find you have made agreements that you later regret. To avoid this "buyer's remorse," you might break rapport by saying, "We've been moving along fairly rapidly, and we seem to have an agreement. Now let's step back and each take a moment to review what our agreement sounds like, looks like, and how we both feel about it so that we can be sure we are making a good arrangement for both of us." Then you may literally step back, increasing spatial distance, while you check out your own see/hear/feel information about the contract. Then and only then would you reestablish rapport.

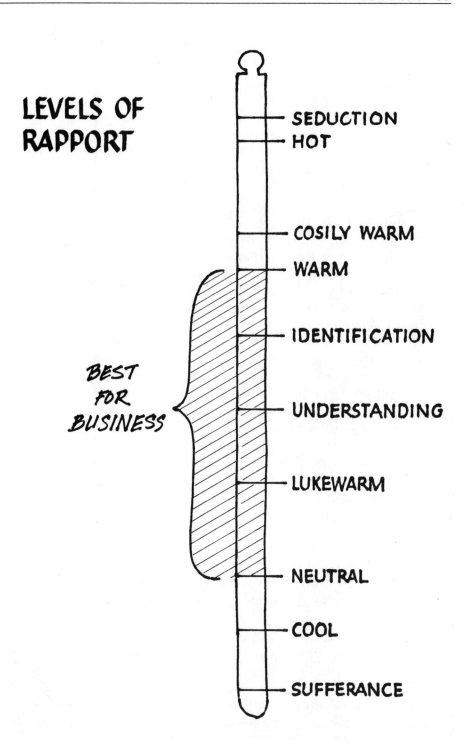

LEVELS OF
RAPPORT

SEDUCTION
HOT

COSILY WARM
WARM

IDENTIFICATION

BEST
FOR
BUSINESS

UNDERSTANDING

LUKEWARM

NEUTRAL

COOL

SUFFERANCE

The power of the rapport techniques became apparent to me when I was brought in as a communication consultant in a delicate negotiation. I received a call one Saturday morning from a distraught stranger, Dave, whose attorney had recommended he learn some negotiation skills from me. Dave explained that he desperately needed to learn these skills over the weekend because he was to negotiate for fees owed him by his former boss.

I explained two days would hardly give me enough time to teach him what he needed. Besides, I was conducting a seminar all weekend.

Dave then insisted that I accompany him to the meeting on Monday. A large sum of money was at stake, and he felt he had the right to bring along a communication consultant.

The negotiation concerned Dave's commissions from land leases agreed to but not finalized before his boss, Mr. Smith, removed him from a project. Dave had not been fired, but he had been transferred to another subsidiary. His contract read that if he were removed from the project, commissions for any lease agreements without final signatures were to be paid or withheld at the discretion of the firm. Smith would make the final decision about Dave's percentages.

Animosity had existed between Dave and Smith for some time, but now it was worse. Dave was justifiably concerned that Smith's animosity would affect how much money Dave received for the leases. Dave had worked on some of these leases for as long as two years and was afraid he would not get any commission.

I met Dave half an hour early on Monday and calmed him down by having him recall *resource states* (memories of times he had felt a sense of confidence). Then it was time to meet with Smith.

Four of us assembled in Smith's office: Dave, Smith, Gail (Dave's former assistant, who was due

RAPPORT

some split commissions), and I. The office was a square fishbowl: two of the glass walls looked out over forests, the other two surveyed fifty cubicles where other employees were at work.

When Smith learned Dave had brought a "professional communicator," he threw a temper tantrum. He yelled, stomped around, and threw papers. He shouted that we would not negotiate while I was in the room. Dave, Gail, and I watched quietly. The people in the cubicles did not look up from their work. After about five minutes, Smith calmed down enough to say I could stay, but I could not say anything. He was still agitated but had stopped yelling and pacing. He dropped into a swivel chair.

I thought about his proposal for a moment, nodded my agreement, then moved to a chair beside Dave. Gail sat on a sofa to one side. I began to match Smith's breathing rate. He was still slightly agitated. Tipping back in his chair, he hooked his heels over its pedestal supports. His legs were akimbo. I was wearing a slim skirt, so I could match only his upper body posture. A few minutes later, I slowed my breathing to a more comfortable rate. Smith followed. At this point, I checked Dave and found that all three of us were breathing with similar rhythms, a sign of rapport among us.

And that is all I did.

By that time, Dave and Smith had negotiated the first contract. Dave got the entire percentage he felt he deserved on all forty leases—a total of almost $100,000. In fact, Gail renegotiated some percentages when she thought Smith was being "too fair" to Dave. On the last few leases, Smith just asked what Dave had been promised, Dave told him, and Smith said, "OK."

At the end of the hour, I shook hands with Smith and said, "I really enjoyed the negotiation, even though I didn't say anything." He consoled me, saying, "Well, listening is an important part of negotiation."

At this point, you know how to set your own out-comes, elicit outcomes from others, and establish rap-port while you explore ways to satisfy both outcomes. You will find mundane conversation becomes an art form as you try out these process-oriented skills.

Once you have practiced these new ways to commu-nicate and find they do work, you will be ready for the next level of communication virtuosity. To help you reach this next level, the next chapter briefly explores connections the brain uses to perceive and organize its perceptions.

All of us have some facility with rapport skills and sensory acuity, but often we use them randomly. By acquiring new skills and focusing on process rather than content, we can substantially increase our effectiveness in communicating.

RAPPORT

PROCESSES OF COMMUNICATION

The processes of communication remain the same across cultures. The content is different.

TALKING _____ SILENCE

LISTENING _____ DISTRACTION

SETTING OUTCOMES _____ BLAMING

CREATING OPTIONS _____ ONE PROGRAM

RAPPORT _____ DISTRUST

PACING _____ RUBBING THE WRONG WAY

LEADING _____ PUSHING

MOVING TOWARD OUTCOMES _____ FRUSTRATION

DOVETAILING OUTCOMES _____ MANIPULATION

PATTERN INTERRUPTION _____ HABITUAL THINKING

STIMULUS-RESPONSE _____ BEING COMATOSE

CREATIVITY _____ AUTOMATIC THOUGHT PATTERNS

SENSORY ACUITY _____ UNAWARENESS

FLEXIBILITY _____ RIGIDITY

CONGRUENCE _____ GETTING IN YOUR OWN WAY

FEEDBACK _____ ABSENCE

CALIBRATION _____ NON REPONSIVENESS

ELICITATION OF OUTCOMES _____ TUNNEL VISION

HUMOR _____ SELF-SERIOUSNESS

METAPHOR _____ CONFRONTATION

PERCEPTION _____ OBLIVION

Deletion, distortion, and generalization affect our maps of reality.

PROCESSES OF PERCEPTION AND THINKING

Deletion occurs when we overlook, tune out, or omit.

Distortion is a personal prejudice that twists our perceptions.

Generalization occurs when we reach a global conclusion based on one or two experiences.

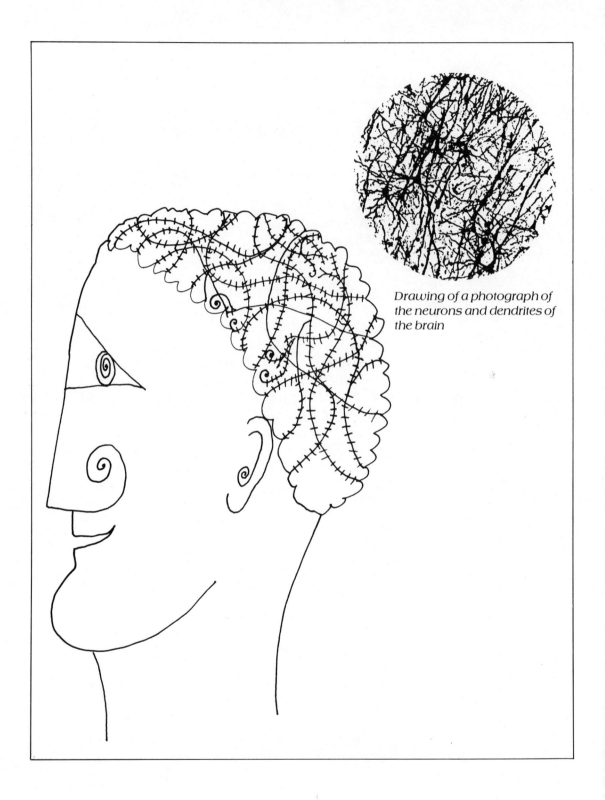

Drawing of a photograph of
the neurons and dendrites of
the brain

3
Perception +
Thinking ⇨
Communication

Before going on any farther in learning about communication, we need to look closely at the relationship between perception, thinking, and talking. What we say is the result of our thinking process. Our thinking process is the result of our present perceptions. These present perceptions may be the result of past or present experiences, or they may be internal or external perceptions about those experiences. Together with thinking, our perceptions determine our communication.

Perceptions are the information gathered by the five senses and processed by the brain. The neurophysiologist C. S. Sherrington referred to the brain as an "enchanted loom." Our perceptions are the warp and the woof, and this loom uses them to create our thought patterns, which it then weaves into the tapestry of our lives. These thought patterns seem even

more enchanted as you learn about the brain and something about how it functions.

Photographed sections of the cerebral cortex show
treelike neurons and dendrites. How one thought makes
its path across the dendrites is as mysterious as magic:
chemicals set up electrical connections through these
neurons, and our thoughts activate these chemicals.
Various chemical combinations transmit our perceptions and thoughts from start to finish. Your response to
the word mother—whether a picture, a sound, or a feeling—is a chemical reaction. Chemical combinations inside the cerebral cortex sort and remember information
from our five senses and the words we use to code
this information.

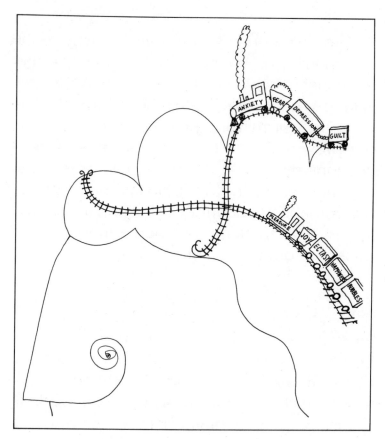

Trains of thought

So the entire process of perception, thinking, and communication depends on combinations of chemicals in the brain. These brain chemicals code and transmit our perceptions and thoughts, which determine our behaviors.

We live in a world filled with many separate objects and people. This is called the "real world." However, none of us operates directly with that world. We use our eyes, ears, nose, tongue, and skin to perceive, then we decide what to do with these perceptions in a process called thinking. Thinking turns perceptions into words.

Do not eat the menu.

Words are a basic way of coding or representing experiences. Language is one way to represent experiences. Language systems represent the total of each person's experiences, just as a menu represents what is available in the kitchen. The words on the menus are symbols for the foods available. The words on our mental maps are symbols for experiences.

For example, if someone walked over and gave you a kiss right now, you would have the experience of being kissed. This is step number one in an interesting process.

You would make a picture of something, hear the smack, feel other lips on yours, generate an emotional response, smell the person's odor, and perhaps taste his or her lips. Step number two.

Then you would make meaning from all those sensations. Step number three.

Next, you would find words to describe the pictures, sounds, feeling, tastes, and smells. Step number four.

The words one chooses to describe an experience often show where generalization, deletion, and distortion occur on one's mental map of reality.

Finally, you ascribe meaning to the words you have selected. Step number five.

You are a long way from the kiss.

"Being kissed" is mostly coded on your mental map during the last four steps. Step number one cannot be coded. By step five, a great deal of deletion, distortion, and generalization has affected the experience of the kiss.

Each person's map differs from the territory it represents, and each person's map differs somewhat from every other map. Alfred Korzybski was the linguist who made this explicit.

Korzybski's basic concepts make it clear that the words we select to describe our outcomes essentially determine whether we obtain those outcomes. When we describe an outcome, we usually use words to describe experiences we have already had and would like to have again, or worthwhile experiences we have seen or heard about.

Transferring a businesslike kiss to a map of reality

These direct or vicarious experiences are recorded in memory by the pictures, sounds, and feelings that were present or fantasized when the experience originally happened. To retrieve these pictures, sounds, and feelings, we often use words. Our brains are organized in such a way that stored sensory representations of an experience, real or imagined, can be retrieved in an orderly fashion from memory by words.

Experience.

Pictures sounds feelings.

Words are representations of the sensory representations—several steps removed from the experience. This representing of representations is where part of the slippage of language occurs. Another slippage is due to the fact that when we mentally file away (code) our sensory experiences, our tendency is to generalize, distort, and delete. Further, when we code in words, we can only code those events for which we already have words. All of these limitations add up to considerable slippage between what we want and the words we use to describe what we want.

Between experience and meanings, five processes affect our maps of reality

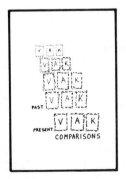

Meaning of VAKs.

Words.

Meaning of words.
Meaning of experience.

Once we have perceived the real world with our senses and coded experiences in our brains on a map or series of maps, then this coding or representation determines our behaviors. Often, people's frustration or unhappiness is the result of limitations in their coding, in their representation of the real world. Sometimes, the very thing to bring about their happiness is available once that thing (or person) is placed on their maps of reality.

Until then, many of us are unable to see or hear the one thing that would make us happy. There may even be several things that could make us happy, or at least content, if only we could expand our map to include these possibilities. The limitations in our perceptions and our thinking processes do limit our choices.

The map determines our behaviors. We determine the map.

Map of reality

Experiences are coded in our brains in pictures, sounds, feelings, smells, and tastes. We call this coding our map of reality.

The maps in our brains are not reality, just as a map is not the territory.

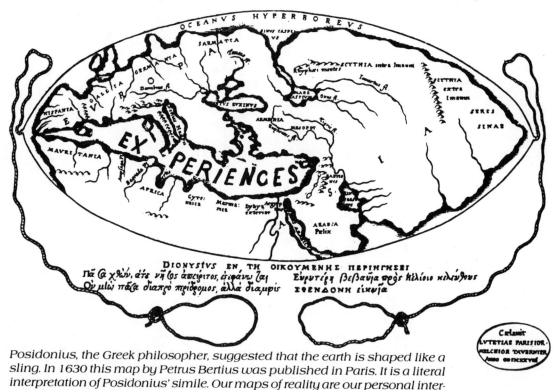

Posidonius, the Greek philosopher, suggested that the earth is shaped like a sling. In 1630 this map by Petrus Bertius was published in Paris. It is a literal interpretation of Posidonius' simile. Our maps of reality are our personal interpretations of experiences mixed with similes and metaphors.

PERCEPTUAL DOORS

The communication process begins with our perceptions. These perceptions are our contact points with the world. As Aldous Huxley pointed out, our senses are like five doors which we open to gather information about the world outside our bodies. Some poets prefer "windows" to "doors" for the eyes, nose, ears, mouth, and skin. The point is that through these, information passes from the outside to our brain.

Our eyes collect pictures, and our ears select sounds. For feelings, we collect both outside (tactile) information and inside information (emotions). Our noses detect odors. For taste, we take parts of the outside world inside our bodies in the process of eating.

Our conscious minds open these doors one at a time—in quick sequence, but sequences nonetheless. Our unconscious minds leave all five doors open all the time and can compute and store more information at each moment than can our conscious minds.

Doors of perception

It is as if each of us were an elaborate television set with five recording devices tuned to pick up five different stations. One station transmits only sound, another only pictures. One sends feelings, and the last two stations send tastes and smells. We have only one screen for our conscious mind. We switch from station to station, favoring one at a time over the others. All the information from the other four channels is being recorded, but not tended to consciously.

Inside this TV set is a little robot who decides what to do by watching and listening to the conscious mind's screen. The conscious mind's decisions are also affected by all the information on the four recorders—information it may never have consciously seen, heard, smelled, felt, or tasted. In fact, most of our perceptions are unconscious. Is it any wonder there are glitches in our decisions and our consequent communication? The unconscious affects our behaviors and communications in curious ways.

> **Most of our perceptions are unconscious.**

Being aware that the unconscious has information not available to the conscious mind is very useful. Just knowing that you and everyone else "know" more than you think you know can make a big difference in communication. You can learn to trust your intuitive impulses and actions. You can have more confidence in your ability to compute the appropriate information available at the moment, and you can feel more comfortable about acting on it.

This knowledge exists unconsciously. Have you ever packed a suitcase, locked your door, and driven off, only to have the nagging feeling of having left something behind? Have you ever gone over a mental checklist? "Not that. No, not that. Yes, I did forget that ... but that's not what is bothering me. Something else, something more important. Oh yes, of course." This scenario is typical of the times your conscious mind is pulling information from your unconscious.

A professor once told me about sitting in his car and suddenly knowing where a treasured gold fountain pen had been hiding for three months: in the crack between

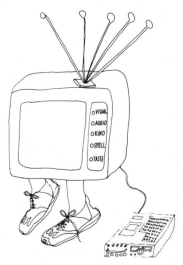

the seat and the center post. He did not suddenly remember that he had never checked that spot. He just knew where it had been. His unconscious had decided to communicate information that his conscious mind had wanted for three months.

REPRESENTATIONAL SYSTEMS

The five doors, windows, or representational systems of perception are: visual, auditory, kinesthetic, olfactory, and gustatory.

Representational systems are the way you perceive and code the memories you bring back from your perceptual trips through the doors.

Which is your favorite door?

What is particularly interesting about human communication is that each of us seems to trust one door more than the others. The door we prefer affects our choice of words. In fact, it affects our breathing, our body posture,

and the way we move our eyes. Most of us seem to select one door of perception as our favorite for certain situations at an early age. Within these situations or contexts, we gather through this door more than the others.

For example, you may have noticed you prefer pictures to sounds. You perceive the sights around you with
your conscious mind and store these pictures as memories. Whenever you see something new, or even something familiar, you refer back to these memories for
meaning. To make sense of your perceptions, you compare present pictures with past pictures. Thus, you know
what a cat is by comparing it with your stored images of
other cats you have seen. When you are in such a situation, using your eyes instead of your ears or your feelings, you are in the *visual mode* of perceiving.

If you prefer sounds to pictures, you will pay more attention to the sounds of the world. Even if you are not a
musician, you will excel at distinguishing subtle differences in sounds. For purposes of discussion, I would describe you as an *auditorily-oriented* individual, since you
trust or prefer your auditory sense.

If you tend to trust your feelings more than pictures or
words, you probably use your conscious mind to notice
the feel of the cat's fur or to compute your feelings (emotions) about, say, cats, people, or modern art. You could
be called a *kinesthetic* or a feeling person. You will be
more aware of tactile feelings and visceral emotions
than either a visual or an auditory.

The smelling and tasting doors are opened in contexts in which these senses contribute useful information: when we are eating or when olfactory stimuli demand attention. Passing a summer garden of sweet
roses or an odoriferous chemical plant, we are suddenly
aware of our ability to detect scents.

In our modern world, olfactory response often re-
mains unconscious. It may, however, affect our daily decisions more than we know. Our attraction or repulsion
to a particular smell could be the result of accessing more information than we are aware of in our conscious minds.

The Category Controversy

Actually, controversy abounds as to whether people can be categorized as having a primary mode. I believe they can. A visual person can use the other modes, but a visual's capacity for discrimination between subtleties in sound, for instance, is more limited than the capacity of an auditory. This capacity to discriminate results from one's life experiences. It is not a permanent limitation. Until the balance of a visual's life experiences changes to the point that his or her map of reality also changes, though, s/he will remain a visual.

An intelligent father who raised his two sons without their mother gave them this advice early on: "When you need to decide yes or no about something, gather all the facts you can, then talk it over with me or someone you respect. After all that, then smell it. If it smells good, do it. If not, don't." His sons still do this, because it works. Their father intuitively gave his sons a decision strategy that used conscious and unconscious information.

We use each of our five senses for conscious information now and then.

People are not totally visual or auditory or kinesthetic, of course. The sense in use depends on the situation, the context. Even if you are attending almost entirely to visual information with all your conscious awareness, sounds and feelings are still being recorded by your unconscious mind.

On a conscious level, we move from door to door in different situations. For this reason, it is not a good idea to classify people as strictly visual, auditory, or kinesthetic. Sometimes it is useful as a flash reading of people. However, people do not use one sense exclusively, and you will only limit yourself if you categorize people this way. Generalizations are useful only if you remember the exceptions are also true.

For the purposes of this book, nonetheless, the terms are sometimes used loosely. When I say that someone is "a visual," let it be understood that I mean that person is using the visual mode at that time and in that context.

Conscious Thought Processes

Communication generally involves more visual, auditory, or kinesthetic information than gustatory or olfactory. The senses of taste and smell can be regarded, for our purposes, as subdivisions of kinesthetic experience. For this reason, and to simplify matters, we will now focus on these three input and memory channels.

In addition, we can further subdivide these three channels into: *visual external,* the door we open to see the outside world; *visual internal,* pictures stored in our memory or imagination; *auditory external,* the door we open to hear words and sounds outside; *auditory internal,* the words, conversations, and sounds stored in our memory or imagination; *kinesthetic external,* the door we open to feel tactile sensations; and *kinesthetic internal,* the memories of tactile sensations and all our emotions, both real and imagined, at this moment and in the past. It is our own personal mixture of all this that comprises our thinking and communication.

One of the difficulties with the door metaphor is that opening and closing doors takes a certain portion of time, even in the imagination, whereas perception, memory, and association seem to happen almost simultaneously. You see a basketball, for example, which evokes the memory of a certain feeling of taut leather and a round shape. The feeling triggers the memory picture of the first basket you ever scored in a game, the sound of the players' voices, and your emotional feeling in response to their words. All this may have happened

Perception, memory, and association seem almost simultaneous.

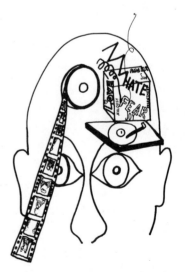

Our true memories are selected pictures, sounds, and feelings which we have edited to fit our belief systems or vice versa.

fifteen years ago, yet the sight of the basketball can bring it back in a twinkling.

To understand thought processes, we need to slow them down and consider each component individually. In the case of the basketball, the conscious mind opened and closed the picture door, then the door for the memory of a tactile feeling; then it ran an old movie with sound track. The movie left you with a feeling from the earlier time. What happened during that movie may determine how you feel about basketballs to this day.

By slowing down and noticing your own thought processes, you can gain deeper understanding of yourself

Memory movies

and the ways you respond to the world in which you live. The words you choose as you respond to your world reinforce certain perceptions and erase others from your conscious mind. Each of us structures the world we live in differently.

Insights into this process can be gained by watching the ways our eyes move as we perceive and think. Eye movements systematically reflect what the brain is doing. Eye movements show whether you are using a visual, an auditory, or a kinesthetic representational system at a particular moment.

Your choice of perceptions and your choice of words both contribute to the structure of your world.

REPRESENTATIONAL SYSTEMS AND EYE MOVEMENTS

A person's eye movements indicate whether s/he is making pictures, listening to internal tapes, or concentrating on feelings. Eyes tend to move up, for instance, when people remember pictures. If you followed our exercise with the basketball, this happened when you were seeing that younger you playing in the game. Your eyes moved down and left when your memory of your teammates' voices became conscious. When you were aware of your emotional response to the game, your eyes probably moved over to the lower right.

Watching this scenario, I could have reported your thought sequence from watching your eye movements. I could not be sure of the content, but I could have gleaned this: when you looked at the basketball, you had a picture of a memory, followed by some remembered words, followed by a feeling. (A visual external picture, a visual internal picture, an internal sound, internal feelings would be the way I would notate this.) I would have missed any remembered smell, because I do not know what way your eyes move in response to a smell. However, simply following your eye movements would give me lots of information about your mental processes at this moment.

You do not know the content, but you can know

Other people's eye movements are like ticker tapes of their ongoing thought processes.

whether someone is using pictures, sounds, or feelings as s/he decides how to respond. This is privileged information, cannot be faked, and is to be treated with respect and courtesy. If you know what internal processes someone is using, you can tailor your words to fit his or her representational system. Certain words are easier for visuals to understand, while other words work best with auditories and kinesthetics. If you match your words to their pictures, sounds, or feelings, they will find you to be an understanding person.

If you attempt to use this information about how other people think to their disadvantage, it will not work. Self-interest overturns any manipulation in the long run,

Eye movements

VISUAL

AUDITORY

KINESTHETIC

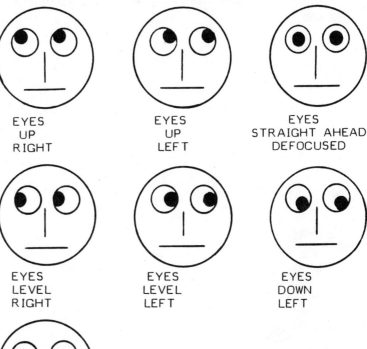

EYES
UP
RIGHT

EYES
UP
LEFT

EYES
STRAIGHT AHEAD
DEFOCUSED

EYES
LEVEL
RIGHT

EYES
LEVEL
LEFT

EYES
DOWN
LEFT

EYES
DOWN
RIGHT

Visuals

Certain external behaviors characterize those persons who are operating, for whatever reason, in the visual mode. The visual person is selecting pictures from memory to make sense of whatever is happening at the time. This happens very quickly. His eyes will be up or, in the case of some individuals, softly defocused but looking straight ahead at a spot about two feet in front of his nose. If you are standing in that exact spot, you may interfere with his memory pictures. He might find this quite irritating; it literally prevents him from thinking. Visuals are also irritated when other people insist on locking eyes and will not allow them to either look up or defocus comfortably.

A visual in an art gallery

The visual's conversation contains a predominance of visual words. Examples are see, clear, and colorful. Visuals use expressions such as, "I see what you mean," and "I get the picture." Their voices may be high-pitched and slightly breathless, for visuals breathe high in the chest. These people often display tension in the neck and shoulders, because tightening here has a tendency to make their pictures more clear. Voice tempo is faster with visuals than with those in the auditory or kinesthetic modes.

Without being able to make pictures, visuals cannot think.

Visuals will recount colors and shapes more extensively than auditories and kinesthetics. They are often deeply affected by the color of their rooms, by the order or chaos of the objects around them, and by sunsets and scenery.

Visuals seldom get lost. If they are in a locale once, they will remember the area and find their way back, especially if they can begin at a familiar point of reference. They collect a lot of internal photographs; even more important, they are accustomed to retrieving these photos. They know how to search their memory files.

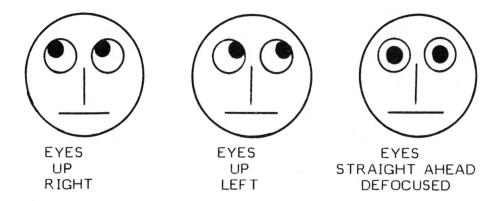

EYES
UP
RIGHT

EYES
UP
LEFT

EYES
STRAIGHT AHEAD
DEFOCUSED

Auditories

People in western cultures use the auditory mode as a primary source of information about the world less often than they use the other two modes. Musicians are auditories, of course. So are radio announcers. Auditories are often proud of their own voices, and for good reason: they are usually melodious. It is important to auditories to sound good. Their voices have a rhythm that is pleasing to them and to others as well.

Auditories often talk to themselves in internal dialogue. They have difficulty making choices because their internal voices go round and round in discussions without knowing how to decide. If auditories would stop talking, either inside or outside, and check out a feeling, they could make a decision; but auditories often do not trust feelings.

An auditory attends a concert

I once had a friend who was an auditory. He loved to talk. A simple question like "How are you?" would evoke a reply quoting Voltaire, Marx, and Mao Tse-tung. One Sunday evening at five o'clock he told me he had spent the entire day debating whether to drive to the coast for dinner. I suggested, "Make a picture of the restaurant, with you sitting on the deck. Now, get a feeling about the picture."

His face broke open, his eyes widened. "I *do* want to go," he said, looking around wildly. Then he looked at his watch. "Oh damn! It's too late. The sun will be set by the time we get there."

At least he could cut off the dialogue.

Auditories tend to breathe in the middle of the chest, lower than the visuals. This gives auditories enough oxygen to have an even, rhythmic tempo, not jerky like visuals or full of blank spaces like kinesthetics.

Auditories use phrases such as "that rings a bell" and "I hear you." If they are experiencing a lot of discord in their lives, they will listen to a record or go to the symphony.

Auditories trust only sounds, and the sounds keep changing.

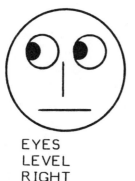

EYES
LEVEL
RIGHT

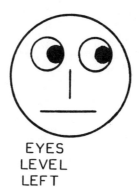

EYES
LEVEL
LEFT

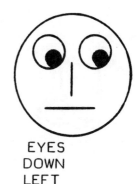

EYES
DOWN
LEFT

Kinesthetics

Kinesthetics breathe low down in the belly, and their voices are deeper than auditories or visuals. The spaces in their conversations give them time to check out their feelings, to get in touch with what is going on. They get a feel for the problem, remove the stumbling block, or untangle the knot. They like or hate and feel warm, cold, or lukewarm about almost everything. True kinesthetics are great in bed, unless they get so carried away with their own responses that they forget their partners.

EYES
DOWN
RIGHT

Kinos wiggle a lot.

A kino gets ready for bed

Cerebrals

Looking around at all the different degrees of response people display leads me to conclude that there may be a fourth category: *cerebrals*. In this category are people who respond not to raw perceptions, but to the labels they give those perceptions. Rather than responding directly, a cerebral names his raw perception and then responds to that name. Cerebrals have a thick filter of language between their perceptions and their responses. We all use language at some point in our perception + thinking ⇨ communication process, but cerebrals seem to introduce word categories early in the process and rely on this language filter to dilute their experiences.

This group includes cerebral-visuals, cerebral-auditories, and cerebral-kinos. It contains the watered-down responders, those people without many external changes in expression and posture who seem to "live in their heads."

Intuitively recognizing that language itself changes our experience, some of us may respond to the experience before we search for words to describe what has happened. Cerebrals do not seem to trust their basic experiences; they trust the words that describe the experiences instead. This gives them their cautious look, as they search for the perfect description.

What eye movements denote a cerebral? The eye movements of this category seem to be the same as those of the visuals, auditories, and kinesthetics. If you are having difficulty picking up a cerebral's eye movements, you could ask an open-ended question such as, "Would you tell me about your best experience with this? What was the most interesting experience you've ever had? What was the best day of your life?" These questions will usually evoke a sequence of eye movements that, along with the cerebral's chosen words, will give you accurate insights into his or her favorite representational system.

> To know what is going on, cerebrals wait until the right label turns up in their thinking process.

You will not be able to detect cerebrals from their eye movements, but from their overall behaviors.

THE CONTEXT

Again, all of us move from mode to mode in different contexts. A businessman may be predominantly cerebral-visual at the office and mostly kinesthetic at home. Typically, his auditory perceptions may be largely unconscious. This seems true for most people. We favor one mode, one door for our perceptions. We sometimes use the second door, but the third stays closed most of the time.

One way to enrich your life is simply to begin opening the third door. You can well imagine that adding a whole new channel of information to your daily activities would be useful. If you go from perceptual door to door, gathering as much data as possible from each, then you can base decisions on various types of data (new pictures, stored pictures, new sounds, old sounds, new feelings, and old feelings). Opening a new door also interrupts your customary patterns of gathering information. This alone is a powerful move toward improving sensory awareness.

Cerebrals respond to the word rather than the sensations.

MATCHING REPRESENTATIONAL SYSTEMS

We live in a world filled with many separate and/or related objects and people. However, none of us operates directly with that world. We use our eyes, ears, noses, mouths, and skin to perceive this world, then we decide what to do with these perceptions. Some we note with our conscious minds; some we do not.

Once we have perceived these objects and people and coded them in our brains, this coding or representation of the real world determines our behaviors. These maps or coding devices are different from the experiences they represent: the experiences are coded in our brains as see/hear/feel/taste/smell sensations. We use these representations to make meaning of the real world in a process called thinking.

Thinking produces the words we use after making meaning of our perceptions. Influencing others in communication becomes easier once you know their favor-

Dated 1538, this map, before my alterations, was attributed to Mercator. The original map is based on Oronce Fine's conception of a heart-shaped design. Fine's idea was based on Johann Werner's projection, but Werner's projection was anticipated by Bernardus Sylvanus in 1511. Our maps of reality are influenced and changed by others, as this one illustrates.

Map of reality

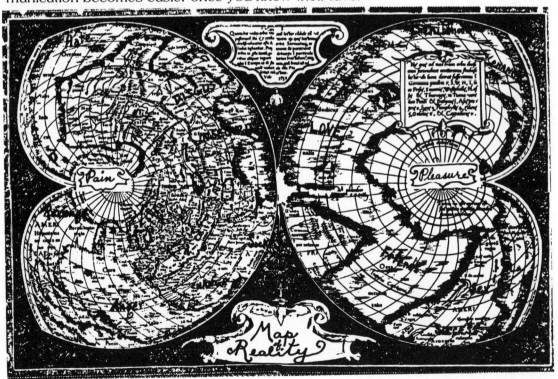

If you choose your words to match a person's favorite system, s/he will find the words meaningful.

ite representational system or which system they are using at this moment. For instance, the simple phrase, "I see what you mean" will be powerful to a visual. "I hear you" or "that rings a bell" will be heard clearly by an auditory. "I grasp what you mean" or "I feel good about that" will convey to a kinesthetic that you understand his position.

Communication becomes easier when you translate your speech into the favorite, familiar representational system of the person with whom you are talking. The translated information slides comfortably into their brain processes instead of having to be changed around or translated in order to be comprehended. You may find that those people who put you at ease immediately are operating in your favorite system. Those with whom you often have conflicts may simply be viewing the same situation from another representational system.

Translation can work wonders.

One of my New York students sat through an entire day of a seminar unconvinced that the material being presented was useful. That night, he received a phone call from a Phoenix business colleague with whom he had a history of conflicts. On most issues, they had had to agree to disagree. He said he usually hung up in frustration. This night, after a few minutes of conversation she said, "I don't get the picture." He remembered that phrase as a typical visual's response. A light bulb went on in his solar plexus (he is a kino).

"Hold on a minute," he replied, going to get his list of words to use with visuals. The picture words did the trick and for the first time they achieved rapport, a decision, and a soft hanging up of the phone.

He arrived at class the next morning with a new expectant attitude, ready to learn anything. He had already copied the accompanying list of representational system words and taped it to his desk top next to his phone.

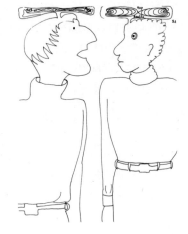

VISUAL	AUDITORY	KINESTHETIC
picture	tune	touch
clear	note	handle
focus	accent	throw
perspective	ring	finger
see	shout	shock
flash	growl	stir
bright	tone	strike
outlook	sing	impress
spectacle	sound	move
glimpse	hear	hit
preview	clear	grope
shortsighted	say	impact
discern	scream	stroke
distinguish	click	tap
illustrate	static	rub
delineate	rattle	crash
paint	ask	smash
cloud	chord	sharpen
clarify	amplify	tangible
graphic	harmonize	crawl
dress up	key	irritate
show	muffle	tickle
reveal	voice	sore
expose	compose	grab
depict	alarm	carry
screen	screech	flat

When you are talking to others, notice where they move their eyes. Up or defocused is for pictures, down right is for feelings, and any place else is for sounds. Then listen to the words they use, determine their favorite system, and translate your way of perceiving the world into their way. It is the polite way to understand and influence others. Remember to keep their outcome in mind as you communicate, so you both can get what you want.

The following pen-and-paper exercise will give you clues about which system is your favorite, which system is second, and which system your conscious mind does not use much. You will find it more difficult to translate and match in this least-used system. Have fun with these. The time you spend on them will pay great dividends within twenty-four hours.

EXAMPLE 1. My future looks hazy.
   Match:
      Visual: When I look to the future, it's not clear.
   Translate:
      Auditory: I can't tune in to my future.
      Kinesthetic: I can't get a feel for what's going to happen.

EXAMPLE 2. Sarah doesn't listen to me.
   Match:
      Auditory: Sarah goes deaf when I talk.
   Translate:
      Visual: Sarah never sees me, even when I'm present.
      Kinesthetic: I get the feeling Sarah doesn't know I'm alive.

EXAMPLE 3. Mary gets churned up on Mondays when the report is due.
   Match:
      Kinesthetic: Mary gets agitated and nervous on Mondays.
   Translate:
      Visual: Mary can't focus on Mondays when the report is due.
      Auditory: Mary hears lots of static on Mondays when the report is due.

Complete the following for increased awareness of representational systems. This is good practice for future use. You'll already be wired to respond when you next hear one of these.

Representational System Practice

1. My boss walks all over me like I'm
   a door mat.
   Match:
   Translate:
   Translate:

2. I get the feeling I'm unappreciated.
   Match:
   Translate:
   Translate:

3. I have trouble looking back to that
   problem.
   Match:
   Translate:
   Translate:

4. I'm guiding this project by the seat
   of my pants.
   Match:
   Translate:
   Translate:

5. She's a sweet girl.
   Match:
   Translate:
   Translate:

6. I ask myself, "How did I ever get
   into this?"
   Match:
   Translate:
   Translate:

7. I can imagine what she's like.
   Match:
   Translate:
   Translate:

8. Something tells me I'm making a
   mistake.
   Match:
   Translate:
   Translate:

9. I've tried to get a handle on what
   my boss means.
   Match:
   Translate:
   Translate:

10. I keep stubbing my toe on
    unexpected obstacles.
    Match:
    Translate:
    Translate:

11. Joe paints a clear picture of
    disaster ahead.
    Match:
    Translate:
    Translate:

12. Smells like a dead fish to me.
    Match:
    Translate:
    Translate:

Before leaving the enchanted loom of the mind and the complex tapestry woven there, let us backtrack over the concepts covered in this chapter.

Our perceptions about the world are coded in the brain. Thoughts using these pictures, sounds, and feelings determine our communication process. Our eye movements follow certain patterns, depending on whether we are using pictures, sounds, or feelings. The words we select for communication reflect our favorite sensory system: visual, auditory, or kinesthetic. By translating our thoughts into the familiar words of another person's favorite representation system, we can increase rapport and understanding.

Drawing by CEM;
c 1961
The New Yorker
Magazine, Inc.

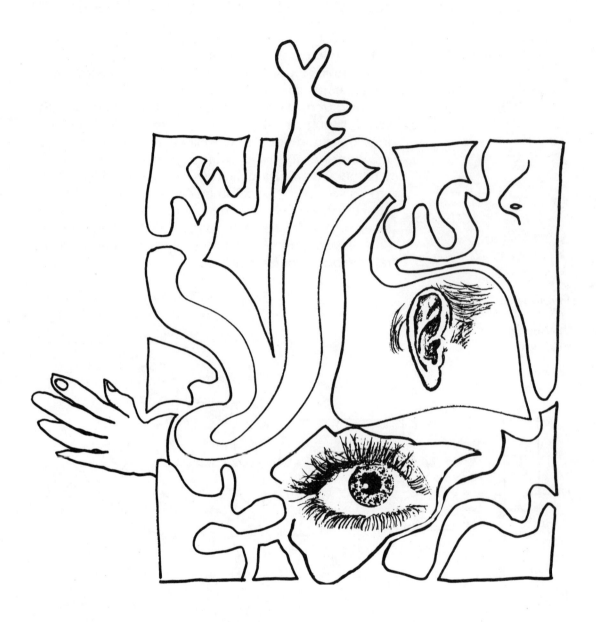

Reality is not fixed. Reality
is a puzzle each of us fits
together. The puzzle has
infinite possibilities and
solutions.

4
Sensory Acuity

We all have some sensory awareness and use it to gain information about others. You have probably passed someone in the corridor of your office building and decided that was *not* the day to ask for an appointment. Increasing this intuitive awareness of others will improve your communication. Also, you will be able to predict with greater accuracy how people will respond to certain communications. Once you are good at predicting, you can pick the words to get the responses you want. Here is an example.

I was having a party one summer in my garden. One of the guests brought a friend whom I had never met. The friend presented me with a bottle of wine as we were introduced.

I thanked him and, bending over, carefully placed it in a tub of ice with other bottles of wine and beer. As I straightened up, his expression stopped me in mid-move. I turned back, pulled his wine bottle out, and said, "Now that I've had a chance to look at the label, I can see this is too special to be treated this way. I'll put it in the refrigerator inside, and we can decide later whether to serve it with dinner." He looked as if he were going to kiss me, he was so relieved to find his gift appreciated.

Once I had seen how distressed he was over my nonrecognition of a special gift, it was easy to predict how to please him. I do not know one wine from another, but I do know how to read conscious and unconscious responses.

The purpose of this chapter is to help you understand how to proceed from sensory awareness to sensory acuity. As the last chapter explained, you can become more acutely aware of sensory feedback by increasing the number of perceptual doors you open. Most people have a door they seldom open (one sense they seldom consciously use). By paying attention to your least-used sense (visual, auditory, or kinesthetic) you can increase your awareness of the information perceived through that door. You can become conscious of a whole new class of data.

First, interrupt your habitual way of gathering information.

You already know how to look someone directly in the eye to see if they are being straight with you. Try something else. Instead of listening to their words, try listening to how they speak. Listen to voice tone and tempo, noticing their shifts, patterns, and emphasis.

You can train your sensory acuity in fifteen minutes a day for a week or two by allowing yourself to look closely and listen carefully. Because we are taught in this culture not to stare or to look closely, we often are unable to see or hear people's many different unconscious responses. These responses cannot be consciously controlled, but neither are they easily perceived by untrained people. Give yourself permission to stare for the next three weeks. When you go to lunch or go to work, stare at other people. Stop if you become too uncomfortable, then select someone new to watch. Most people will ignore you. Even if people think you are a little strange, the benefits are well worth it.

Changes are responses, and any change in a person during the communication process is important to notice.

Eye Accessing Cues = Rep System Clues

Rapport

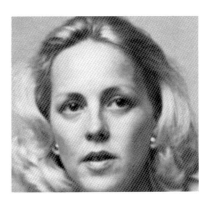

Matching and leading to a more receptive state.

Muscle Tone Changes

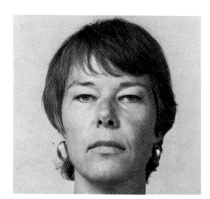

Gross changes are easy to spot. Subtle changes are more difficult until you have trained your eyes to notice. Here are two examples of muscle tone changes. See what differences you are aware of, then notice specific areas on the next page.

Skin Color Changes

C

Skin Color Changes

D

These photographs were made in a studio with a Nikon F3 using electronic flash, Kodachrome 25 color transparency film, and a 105mm F2.5 Nikkor lens.
Baron Wolman
Mill Valley, California

Skin Color Changes

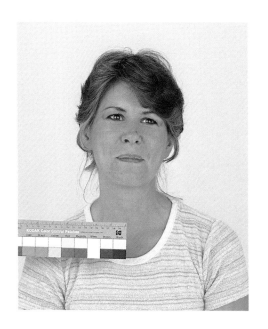

F

Muscle Tone Changes

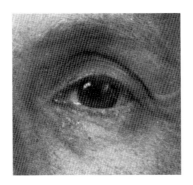

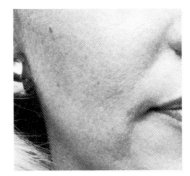

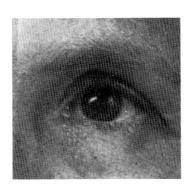

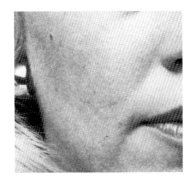

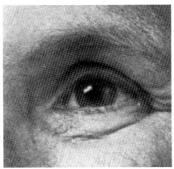

The changes in muscle tension around the eyes provide a wealth of information.

You may find clues in any muscles you can see. In this example, notice the changes in the tone of the cheek muscles.

Lower Lip Changes

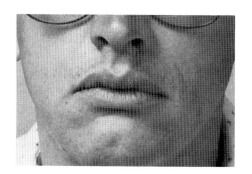

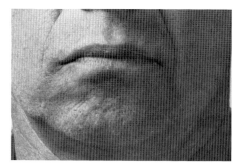

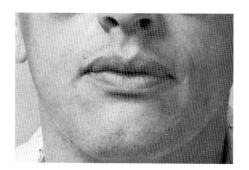

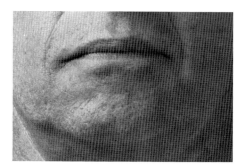

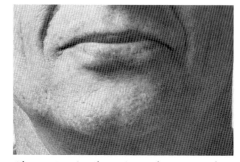

Changes in the size, shape, color, and tension of the lower lip can give you valuable information for determining internal states.

What are you going to be looking for? Changes. The other person is responding if s/he shows any change. *Our internal response is reflected systematically in our external behavior.* Our thought patterns, our neurons and dendrites firing, cause consistent responses in our faces and bodies. Internal thoughts and emotions show up in external expressions and body postures. The same thoughts trigger the same external responses in a given person (*not* the same responses as in other people).

Most of us have not been trained to see these responses unless they produce large changes. Misunderstandings are often the result of incorrectly interpreting what few responses we do see—the clenched jaw, the blush, or the crossed arms—and overlooking the more subtle responses in muscle tone, breathing rate, minute shifts in the lower lip, or slight changes in skin color.

Interpreting changes in other people is a dangerous pitfall. We all seem to fall into this. That is, we assign meanings to their responses based on our own experience. When I wrinkle my forehead, it means one thing. When you do it, it may mean something totally different.

If sixteen people are in a room, they will have sixteen different ways of coding reality and responding. Eventually, when you have studied a person long enough and with sufficient sensory acuity, you will be able to guess what his or her responses mean. Once you have collected enough data to make a guess, check out your interpretation with the other person. Otherwise, you may find yourself going down the road all alone. Slow down, look, listen and intuit. You can interpret later. This is important to keep in mind while you are learning to see, hear, and feel in new ways.

Another way to increase your sensory acuity is to pretend you are compiling a scrapbook of photographs of the person you are with at the moment. You can take imaginary photos and store them in your memory very quickly. You will know you have enough photographs when you begin to see patterns among them. Patterns are repetitions, differences, rhythms, and changes. For

I cannot use my own experience to decide what your change means to you.

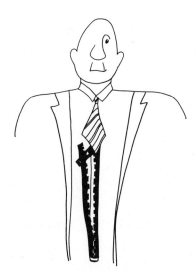

What is going on inside consistently shows up outside, at least minimally.

example, when the other person is feeling anxious, he may shift his weight and pull on his ear. His face may have pale splotches. At that point, when you begin to see patterns, you can also begin to check out the meanings of the patterns. For example, you can ask "Were you feeling anxious when you said, 'No sugar, thanks'?" To yourself, you can add, "And you had pale splotches, a weight shift, and an ear pull."

UNCONSCIOUS VISIBLE RESPONSES

If you begin to notice things you have never noticed before and refrain from interpreting what these changes mean, you will make a giant step forward in influencing with integrity. Sensory acuity is the most important and far-reaching skill you can learn. Here are the four unconscious responses to watch in others.

- Skin color changes
- Minute muscle changes
- Lower lip changes
- Breathing changes

Most people find these responses fairly easy to see, once they have been pointed out. Then, too, since these four responses are unconscious, they remain outside the subject's conscious awareness and so convey "straight," undiluted information.

Many other physiological changes occur besides the four listed above, of course. As we talk, body postures shift in ways both great and small. Weight shifts, head tilts, shoulders moving up or down, necks stretching, and hand gestures are parts of the patterns of response.

While you are learning, these obvious responses will be easier to see then the subtle ones. Fairly soon, you may want to begin looking for the slighter responses as well. The great medical hypnotist Milton Erickson watched pulse changes, for example. Friends have noticed how the blonde hairs on my arm stand up or lie flat, depending on my emotional state. And one of my students reported that he had watched ear lobes for years.

Unconscious visible responses are true indicators of the person's emotional state.

Very responsive, ear lobes: They show color changes, tension, and relaxation. The best part is nobody suspects what you are up to or that you are watching.

Skin Color Changes

When Picasso, Braque, and the other artists painted faces in triangles, squares, and circles, they may have been responding to the different colors in the planes of faces. Certainly the colors are there. Once you begin looking, you may be amazed that you never noticed all this kaleidoscopic color before.

If you are an artist, you already know about the subtle colors in the complexions of people, whether they are brown, black, white, red, or yellow. When I was a child and learned about the colors of mankind, I pictured bright red faces and lemon yellow faces in faraway lands. I had seen black and white, but the others were colored in my child's imagination. If you can adopt this free imagination, you can quickly see blue, green, grey, lavender, pink, and yellow in the faces around you.

The color changes are easier to see if you think of contrast. Contrast the nose color with the skin color of the forehead. Which is more pink? Contrast the triangle at the ends of the eyes with the half moon under the eyes. Once you can see the contrasts of the different sections of the face, you can begin to notice the changes. Blushes, of course, are easy. These color changes are more subtle than blushes. You will find speckles of color appear and disappear.

After a surprisingly short time, you will be able to detect and calibrate which colors signify which internal states or processes. You may say to yourself, "Whoops, her forehead is alabaster with green tinges near the hairline. Her nose is rose with pink and grey around the nostrils. Her skin at the ends of her lips is yellow-grey. She's thinking of making an apple pie for dinner." Or "She's going to accept my proposal." Or "She's flying off to Paris. There's her Paris palette."

Paris evokes a strong, distinct response in many people. Go out and discover the pattern of color response for Paris in one of your friends. Or several friends. You can talk about Paris, get them involved, then switch to Minneapolis. Notice the color change. You do not need to pay attention to content, so you can watch color changes. Once you have found some color shifts, notice the tension and relaxation in the small muscles around the mouth.

Subtle behavior changes are communication.

Minute Muscle Changes

Tension and relaxation play over the small muscles of the face. These shifts are the most obvious at the outer corners of the eyes, around the mouth, and at the jaw line. Sometimes the nose becomes "sharper." The deepening of a crease between the eyes or up across the forehead may also indicate an internal change.

These small muscle changes are idiosyncratic to individuals: their meanings are not universal. With some practice and feedback, you can learn to detect small facial changes and correlate them with the individual's communication process and perceptions. Eventually, you will be able to detect muscular tension and relaxation throughout the body.

Lower Lip Changes

Look at the lower lip of your communication partner as you interact. Gather as many "photographs" as you can of this lip so you can begin to see patterns: repetitions, differences, similarities, and gross changes in the size, shape, texture, movement, trembling, firmness, color, wetness, and tumescence.

Lower lips are difficult, if not impossible, to control consciously. You are perceiving signals straight from the unconscious of the other person. You can interpret these signals accurately after you have enough mental photographs. After a short while, you can connect certain photographs with the words being spoken at the same time. Then you can add labels to the photographs.

Breathing Changes

You cannot know what this shift means until you have learned the entire pattern and connected a particular pattern to a particular internal state, such as anger or fascination, curiosity or impatience.

As discussed in the chapter on rapport, the most important thing to remember is that if you cannot see the up and down movement of breathing in chest and abdomen, do not despair. Shift your attention to the edge of the shoulder and wait. You will begin to see the breathing response.

People breathe high in the chest, low in the chest, at the waist, and deep in the abdomen. They breathe fast, slow, medium, with pauses, and in various rhythms. If the breath changes as you converse, there has been a physiological shift. Remember, this differs from person to person. One thing is sure: when the breathing shifts in rhythm or in body placement, something has changed for this individual.

When you are astute in your observations, you will begin to know the answer to your question before the person can reply. And when you have successfully guessed five answers, you have made the first step toward *calibration.* Calibration is the recognition of a certain state in a person by nonverbal signals.

Calibration is a key to successful communication.

You are also learning what fortune-tellers see in their crystal balls. They "see" the correct answers to their predictions in the responses to their words, and they change their magical revelations until they get the yes response: "I see a dark . . . no, the mist is clearing . . . a dark blonde m———no, it's a woman wearing slacks. This fair woman is driving . . . no, actually she is riding . . . a bicycle! Yes, a bicycle."

Each person's responses are different, so avoid generalizing. Practice your calibration with at least three people before moving on to the next exercise.

 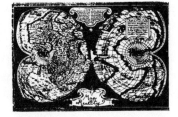

Sensory Acuity

To learn sensory acuity more easily, try these exercises with a friend. If you take time in the next few weeks to do these, you will find yourself seeing and hearing more than you thought possible. You will know a lot more about what is going on with your friends and your enemies. With this extra information, you may also find enemies become friendlier, if you wish. You may even find yourself feeling more friendly as your own awareness increases.

EXERCISE 1. THE LIVING LIE DETECTOR

Find someone willing to play with you. This exercise will be easier with someone you do not know very well— an acquaintance rather than a close friend, a coworker rather than a spouse.

Tell this person you are going to ask a series of questions and s/he is to answer yes or no.

Ask three questions you know will be answered yes. For example, if your partner is John Smith, a married man living in Anytown with his wife, Ethel, and one dog, a poodle, you might ask:

Is your name John Smith?
Do you live in Anytown?
Are you married?

Then ask three questions you know will be answered no, such as:

Is your name Fred Perkins?
Is your wife's name Mildred?
Do you have four dalmations?

Your task is to watch the changes in facial expression, body posture, and breathing as your partner finds the answer. Notice and remember all the unconscious visible responses to the yes questions and compare them to those for the no answers. Be aware of the differences in breathing, skin color, lower lip, and minute muscle movements.

Continue to alternate yes and no questions until you feel confident you know the difference in that person's responses. When you are sure you can tell the difference, start asking questions to which you do not know the answers. For example:

Did you major in science?
Did you wear your hair long when you were twenty?
Have you always wanted to go to Istanbul?
Is your mother older than your father?
Did you once own a motorcycle?

"Guess" the answers using your newfound "extra" sensory perception. Then check them out.

EXERCISE 2. THE TELL-TALE LOWER LIP

Devote an entire day to watching lower lips. Every moment you can snatch from your duties is to be dedicated to lower-lip surveillance. Focus on the changes in the lower lip of everyone you talk to that day. Do not attempt to decide what the different configurations mean. Just notice the shifts in size, color, shape, edges, engorgement, flattening, stretching, curving up, or turning down. After some time in this strange pursuit, you will notice the minute changes that signify patterns of unconscious response.

EXERCISE 3. THE WILD COLOR PALLETTE OF SKIN

Take a day off and try *not* to notice lower lips. Then go for colors you have never noticed before. Pretend you are Picasso. Begin to notice small areas of color in faces that used to look pink or cream or brown. Now, with the imagination of Picasso, you can begin to see that faces are not all one color. Not only do faces have splotches and dots of grey, green, lavender, and yellow, but the colors also change and shift around as people talk. Pretend you are painting a color portrait of each person you meet. What colors do you see?

If, at the end of day one of color acuity, you have noticed ten splotches of colors you would not have seen the day before, move on to exercise 4. If you have picked up less than ten, stay in the Picasso role another day or so.

Increasing your color perception is sometimes difficult. Sometimes it helps to imagine what colors might be there. In any event, after three days as Picasso, move on.

EXERCISE 4. MINUTE MUSCLE MOVEMENTS
Anyone can see a scowl or a smile, but to see the small changes in the jaw, at the corners of the mouth, and around the eyes takes more skill—skill that must be learned. Learning sensory acuity is like learning to play a piano. You learn each note, then learn sequences and combinations; finally, after much practice, you become a pianist. One day of focusing on minute muscle changes may be enough, or it may take two days for you to be good enough to move on to recognizing breathing shifts.

EXERCISE 5. SPIRIT WATCHING
The Greeks thought the breath and the spirit were one and the same. You can tell a lot about the spirit by watching the patterns of breathing and their changes. Take at least one day to focus on breathing. If you work where men and women wear suits, you may need to watch the top edge of their shoulders as they rise and fall. Many layers of clothes make the breathing more difficult to follow. When you are an expert on spirit watching, you will be able to use this skill to great advantage in the exercises on rapport. Our breathing reveals a lot about our responses to any situation.

EXERCISE 6. TUNING IN TO SOUNDS

A good way to learn more about the sound of the voice and the meaning of changes in tempo, tone, and volume is to listen to a radio or television station broadcasting in a language you do not understand. You cannot get sidetracked by the content of the news, and you can place all your attention on the sounds themselves. Begin by noticing the tempo—how fast or slowly the people are speaking. Are there pauses? Long or short? Consistent or irregular?

After you have listened for a time, begin to guess what the tempo is

saying about the content. Notice the shifts in tempo and guess the reason for these shifts. You may be right or wrong. This doesn't matter. What matters is that you are learning to hear shifts you would not have noticed earlier and to recognize that the shifts have meaning inside the communication process. Later, when you practice listening to voice sounds with friends, you can check out your guesses to find out how often you are on target.

Once you have caught the tempo of the radio or TV announcers, you can hum right along with their tempo, making nonsense sounds at the same rate they are using. Once you have the tempo, you can match tonal and volume shifts as well.

After you are satisfied that you can hear tone, tempo, and volume and can match these well enough to feel pleased, you are ready for the next step.

You now bring your new skills of matching tone and tempo to an American radio or TV broadcast. Ignoring content, try out your new skills. Within a short time, you will be able to listen to content and match tempo with a hum at the same time. Your goal is to match tempo and tone and to listen to content, all at once or in a quick sequence. It is possible, and you will profit from being able to do this.

EXERCISE 7. VOICE MATCHING

For this exercise, you need a friend who would also like to increase his or her sensory acuity. S/he tells you a three-minute story and you listen. Then you tell the same story in the same tone, tempo, and volume s/he used. The content is less important than the sound matching.

A third person is useful for this exercise. The third person can give you feedback on how close you were in matching. If a third person is not available, the two of you can learn a lot by alternately telling and matching. Continue until you feel satisfied with your performance in voice matching.

If this exercise seems too difficult at first, retell the story to the back of your friend's head so you do not get distracted by his or her facial expressions. Another way to make it easier is to match the story in nonsense syllables or by humming so you do not have to bother with content.

Your goal is to handle content at the same time as you match tempo, tones, and volume.

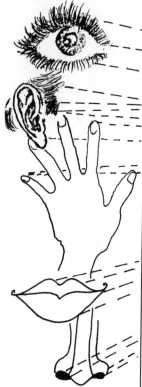

WE
SELECT
WHAT
WE

SEE
HEAR
FEEL

BENEFITS OF SENSORY ACUITY

Having a heightened ability to notice sensory changes in others enables you to recognize when your communication partner is responding to you and your outcomes.

Why develop your sensory acuity? It is the foundation for the art of communication. You need sensory acuity to establish rapport. You need it to know when you have lost rapport. You need sensory acuity to read the road signs that will lead you to your destination. Some signs tell you that you have made a wrong turn and need to turn around, if you want to gain your outcome. Being able to recognize that you have gone off the road and are heading for a ditch is very useful when you are in an intricate communication. You can, with improved sensory acuity, notice that you need to do something to avoid the ditch.

The wonderful thing about increased sensory acuity is that you will know almost as soon as your partner knows that something has shifted. If the shift is useful for dovetailing outcomes, then you can increase whatever you did to cause the shift. If the change is not useful in dovetailing outcomes, then you have been warned by the other to change what you are doing into something that does work.

When you are communicating, you want to be in the best state possible to gain your outcomes. You want your partner in an optimum state to be able to gain his or hers. With sensory acuity, you can recognize this state of excellence and be able to evoke it at will. With sensory acuity, you can acquire the potential to leave everyone in a better state than when you first met.

Evoking another's optimum state is the polite way to communicate.

We have separated the skills leading to communication excellence into short segments of instruction, and we have structured the exercises so you can weave them into your daily activities, but you may need to spend more than three minutes a day practicing each skill. The rewards are often instantaneous and may be great enough to entice you to break patterns of a lifetime in order to get your outcomes. If you keep doing the same thing, you will keep getting the same old results. Try out the new ways of seeing, new ways of hearing, and enjoy your new outcomes.

5
The Five
Finger Pointers

The time has come to deal with words and what they may mean in a particular communication process. The words are the *content* of communication. Until now we have been concerned with the *process* of communication, not the content. The content is much less important than facial expressions, body postures, and the sounds of the voice (tone, timbre, tempo, volume) according to linguistic experts like Mehrabian and Birdwhistell. Yet content does matter, and we do need to understand what the other person is saying. Mutual understanding becomes especially important in a business meeting, whether the meeting is between two people or twenty. The next chapter gives procedures to cut down your meeting time. To use these procedures, you need to know about five questions called the Pointers.

The Pointers have a distinguished lineage.

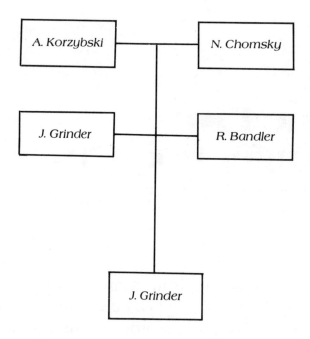

Their great-grandparents are Alfred Korzybski and Noam Chomsky. Korzybski pointed out that the map of something is not the same as the territory it represents, and the word is not the thing named. We all know that the word cat is not the same thing as a furry, white, purring kitten, but sometimes we forget that the "map" word of cat is insufficient to deal with all the panthers, bobcats, tigers, and lions that may inhabit the territory.

Chomsky added the idea that impoverished and inadequate mental maps of reality are the result of glitches (malfunctions) in our perceptual and thinking processes.

John Grinder and Richard Bandler became the grandparents of the Pointers when they took these earlier ideas, added new insights, and created the Meta Model to explain how language works. The explanations of Korzybski and Chomsky are so involved that their ideas were not too useful until Bandler and Grinder came up with the Meta Model. Originally, the Meta Model filled two books, volumes I and II of *The Structure of Magic.* John Grinder became the Pointers' parent by single-handedly reducing these two books to five questions.

These five questions, the Pointers, are the most useful set of words you will ever learn.

That is a strong statement. I believe it is true. If you want to find out what another human being really means by his communication and how his thought processes are affecting his behavior, these five questions are the answer.

The first two Pointers clarify nonspecific nouns and verbs. The third Pointer questions rules like "shoulds" and "should nots." The fourth Pointer is for generalizations. The fifth is for changing comparators without antecedents (such as "better").

SYNTONIC LEARNING

In learning about the five Pointers, I also invite you to use a new way to learn, a way that engages your three major senses: seeing, hearing, and feeling. This process of accelerated syntonic learning is based on discoveries about how people learn easiest through associated experience. By engaging all three senses, you can learn the Pointers quickly. Both the recognition of when a Pointer would be useful and the appropriate question will become automatic, like riding a bicycle or turning the steering wheel of your car.

If you play tennis, you know that when you see a tennis ball coming, you just swing, seemingly without a

Map of reality

Another map of reality

thought going through your head. The learning seems to be lodged in your body. If you participate in the exercises on the next few pages, you can lodge this new information about Pointers in your fingers, so that your fingers can do the thinking without bothering your head. Automatic responses to language mysteries will free your mind for other matters when communicating.

POINTER 1: NOUNS

The first Pointer is used to define nouns. Dictionaries do not define nouns absolutely; they merely deceive us into thinking that words have definite meanings. Because of the way our brains store information, though, these "definite" meanings are modified by our past experiences and our future expectations. Dictionary meanings therefore are of limited value in daily conversations: any one noun has as many definitions as there are people using the noun.

If three people are discussing "productivity," for example, this word has three meanings. One person may be considering the hours of productivity; the next, the people involved; and the third, the machinery of productivity. So if you hear "increased productivity"—or "this year's profits," or "end result," or any indefinite noun—you will need Pointer Number 1 to ensure that everyone is both sure of the meaning and sure that the other people share this meaning for the moment.

The Pointers are questions. To recognize the need for Pointer 1, you must be able to recognize an unspecified noun. First you will teach your fingers the recognitions. Then you will learn the Pointer questions.

Use Pointer 1 on unspecified nouns.

Step 1: Recognition

Place your left hand over the drawing of a left hand. Then lift your forefinger as you imagine the word noun printed on the finger; simultaneously, say noun out loud.

Recognition hand*

*The thumb is unmarked to indicate the relative unimportance of Pointer 5, the comparator.

RECOGNITION HAND

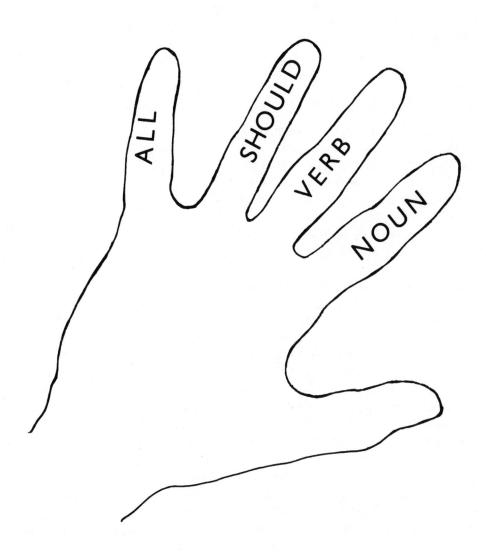

If this is too much like rubbing your stomach and patting your head at the same time, then do the lifting, saying, and imaginary visualization in a quick sequence. Do this three times.

Step 2: Response

Place your right hand over the drawing of a right hand. Lift your forefinger while saying the question, "What noun, specifically?" at the same time, imagine "What?" printed on the lifted forefinger.

Step 3: Recognition-Response

Place both hands over the correct hands on the drawing. (Don't worry—nobody's watching.) Lift the forefinger of your left hand, imagine "noun" printed on the finger, and run the sequence of saying noun out loud, then lift your right forefinger and say, "What noun, specifically?" as you imagine "What?" printed on that finger. One time may be enough to set this stimulus-response connection in your neurology, If not, three times will probably do it.

Now, if this learning has indeed become automatic, this is the sequence of events: your left forefinger twitches because an unspecified noun has appeared in someone's communication. Your right forefinger jerks and immediately the question pops into your head: What noun, specifically?

For example, your assistant says, "I want a new job." When you have learned the sequence, your fingers will respond, and you will naturally reply, "What job, specifically?"

Whether you ask the question out loud at the point the unspecified noun occurs or you wait until a more appropriate moment depends on the circumstances. Your own common sense will advise you about the timing. If you decide to wait a bit, remind yourself that you do not know what this noun means to the other person, and re-

*Pointer hand**

**The thumb is unmarked to indicate the relative unimportance of Pointer 5, the comparator.*

POINTER
HAND

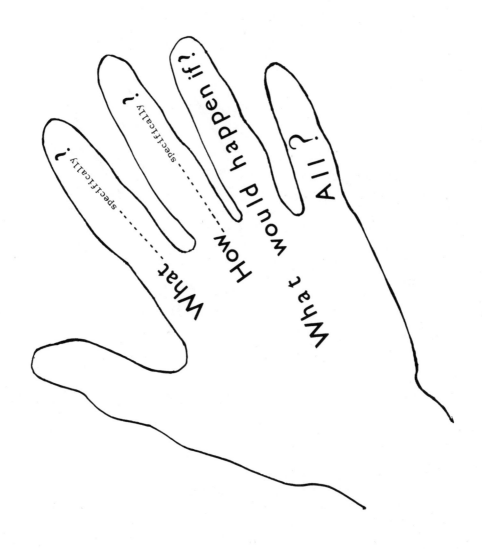

mind yourself to find out his or her specific meaning for this word as soon as appropriate.

Even if you can make a good guess, do not count on this guess. Remember, we all have different experiences in our memories, and these experiences are what give meaning to our words. Our maps of reality are different. The same words mean different experiences to different people, and herein lie many of the problems of communication. The five finger Pointers, if used often and gracefully, will untie the knots of communications.

POINTER 2: VERBS

The second Pointer is to be used with verbs. Once the fat on all the nouns has been pared away, the verbs come next. To learn and automate this Verb Pointer quickly, find the recognition chart and go through the same moves with the middle fingers and unspecified verbs as you did with unspecified nouns: twitch the left middle finger with the word verb, then ask the question, "How (verb), specifically?" When you have done this three times, your fingers will have learned how to use the first two Pointers. If not, continue this sequence for a few minutes, until you make this new connection.

An example of the Verb Pointer:

Use Pointer 2 on unspecified verbs.

"I will prepare this report by the 12th." Your response, after a finger twitch or two, would be, "How, specifically, would you prepare the report?" You may be looking for a verbal report, and your employee may be planning to have it typeset with graphs and color illustrations—who knows? Your employee knows. It is better you find out now, not on the 12th.

The first two Pointers uncover specific meanings that are idiosyncratic to the individual. The next two Pointers are not for stripping down fat words to lean words but are spotlights to illuminate holes, blanks, or glitches in your or the other person's thinking processes. Most of us

Recognition hand and pointer hand

have thinking habits that are less than optimal. Deletions, distortions, and generalizations are errors on our maps of reality that often block us from seeing answers to our problems. Often the answers are clear to someone else. Have you ever had the experience of relating a problem to a friend who immediately came up with a new option you had not thought of? The next two Pointers can be your friends in just this way.

PRODUCTIVE

POINTER 3: RULES

You will need a friendly Pointer when you meet a "should" or a "shouldn't," a "must" or a "musn't," a "have to," a "can't," or an "ought." Called *modal operators* in linguistics, these words indicate rules that may or may not be legitimate. Rules and limitations are fences we build around our possible actions. Outside the fence—outside our awareness—are other possible behaviors which we ignore once we accept the given limitation. The rule becomes as absolute as the sun rising in the east; it is an accepted part of the world, even though it may have been established by a supervisor who accepted it based on a policy written in 1890.

Written or unwritten, rules should be evaluated now and again to see if they are still necessary and appropriate. Invalid rules waste time and materials, which ultimately costs your firm money. So teach your ring finger to recognize a "should" just as you taught the other fingers to respond to unspecified words. Find the charts, position your hands, and continue the learning process as before. Simply twitch your ring finger as you say to yourself, "should" and "should not," three times in a row. Imagine "should" printed on your finger. Twitch, "Should,

Use Pointer 3 on should, should not, must, must not, have to, cannot, ought to, ought not.

should not." Twitch, "Should, should not." Twitch, "Should, should not."

The Pointer question that challenges "should" statements is: "What would happen if you didn't?" The Pointer question that responds to "should nots" is: "What would happen if you did?" Be sure to add these questions to your automatic twitch. "Should"/"What would happen if you did not?"

You are now prepared to handle one of the most insidious ways we limit our actions. "Shoulds" and "must nots" are red flags indicating our thinking processes have limited our behaviors in ways that may or may not be legitimate. The third Pointer quickly checks out the validity of the limitation and may add amazing choices for you and any friends to whom you loan this Pointer.

A business example is, "We must always get the financial report out on the first." Third Pointer: "What would happen if we didn't?"

By questioning the rules of others and the rules we have taken into our reality, we have new options and choices.

A word of caution: use these last two Pointers on your own thinking processes any time, but use great discretion when using them on another's language. For example, this conversation could get you into trouble:

"You can't have three weeks for vacation."

"What would happen if I did?"

Remember to entertain both your short- and long-term goals. The above response could get you a permanent vacation.

Used appropriately, the third Pointer is powerful in communicating for outcomes and for increasing your own options. You may decide to look for a job that offers a three-week vacation. Or you may find ways to increase the efficiency of your operations. At one law firm, for example, one of the secretaries always stopped her type-written pages twenty spaces from the bottom edge. She was efficient, and after some years became office manager and supervisor of the typists' pool. The typists who worked under her copied her format. Ten years later, a curious new typist asked why all the legal-size documents had such wide bottom margins. Nobody knew. Finally, someone asked the office manager. She laughed

shoulds

and said, "Oh, ten years ago our copying machine would not copy legal-size pages."

The ring finger Pointer for this situation would be, "What would happen if we typed the whole page?"

Here are more examples of how the third Pointer can be used. "Company policy is that we check in at this time clock at 8 in the morning, out at 12, in at 1, and out at 5." "Company policy" is a synonym for "should." What would happen if we didn't? If people were not treated like machines, productivity might increase. Or productivity might decrease. Unless you ask the question, though, the options go unexplored.

Here is another accepted "truth": "To be successful in business, it is necessary to go to college." What would happen if you didn't? I know someone who made a million dollars in real estate during the years his parents were trying to send him to college. He is now educating himself, in luxury.

Like any powerful tool, the third Pointer is dangerous if misused. When the Pointers were still known as the Meta Model, one of its originators, John Grinder, taught a course in linguistics at the University of California at Santa Cruz. The class heard rumors about these great new tools and asked for a special presentation to learn them. When the class met on Friday, Dr. Grinder taught them about the Meta Model, which was too new to be a part of the curriculum. He warned them that the questions are potent and must be used on others with great sensitivity.

The students did not heed his words. When they came in the next Monday, they were dejected, depressed, and desperate. Over the weekend, they had unleashed the questions on their friends and loved ones and had alienated almost everyone of importance in their lives.

Softeners: I'm wondering..., I'm curious..., Would you be willing...

These questions are pointed, like lances or the verbal jousts of a cross examination. People do not take kindly to having the limitations in their thinking exposed. Use the Pointers with rapport, and pay attention to the other person's response. Stop when you notice anger in another, unless you want to deal with anger. If that is your outcome, the Pointers are ideal. If you want to keep your supervisors and your job, add softening phrases such as:

"I'm wondering what, specifically, you mean by————."

"I'm curious about————."

"Would you be willing to tell me how, specifically, to————?"

Then watch carefully to see what responses the Pointers elicit in the other person. Remember always to maintain rapport. Without it, no communication will ever be entirely successful.

POINTER 4: GENERALIZATIONS

The fourth Pointer works to expose the fallacy of *generalizations*. Generalization is a natural thinking process that makes it possible for us to open doors and turn door-knobs without thinking. Once we know what one door is for and how one doorknob turns, we generalize this information to all doors and simply open them without a thought. Our bodies, our hands, learned about doors and we then generalized this information. Obviously, we need generalizations to function in the world. It would be inconvenient to have to learn how to open a door each time we confront a doorknob.

On the other hand, inappropriate generalization can create unnecessary pain and limitations in behavior. We generalize when we have one or more experiences and decide that all future experiences with similar character-istics will duplicate the same scenario. For example, if three supervisors are rigid and stern, we may decide that all supervisors are rigid and will cause us head-aches. No matter how many flexible and friendly supervi-sors we encounter, we may feel dread at the sight of any boss.

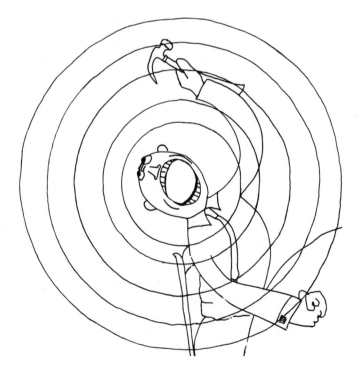

Generalization: All bosses are difficult, if not impossible.

The same generalization process may occur when a corporation reduces its work force and we find ourselves out of a job. This generalization may prevent us from taking the risk of being laid off ever again.

A generalization can also expand a specific fearful experience to the point where one feels persecuted by the entire universe and everything in it. This is an extreme response, of course. More common are responses like these: "I can't find a job where I'm appreciated" or "I'm better off on welfare than risking a pink slip."

The little-finger Pointer can reconnect a person to the present experience, adding detail and richness to one's thinking. Richness of sensory data adds choices based on awareness—choices perhaps not available within a generalization.

Words such as all, every, and always will alert you to generalizations. Essentially, these words lie. Few generalizations are true all the time. When we generalize, we ignore the exceptions to the rule. And in these excep-

Our own generalizations often distort our maps of reality and prevent us from making distinctions—this friendly supervisor or that growing corporation—that could give us a fuller set of choices in any given situation.

Generalization: All men kiss and tell.

Generalization: All women will; some you have to marry.

tions are the overlooked options of behaviors. Generalizations are always limiting. Always? Not always. The generalizations of all, every, and always can block off avenues of escape from problems, avenues that offer unexamined or unnoticed solutions.

"Never" is another generalization that limits. "We never promote women to senior level," for example, should raise a couple of fingers. Your ring finger may move and a voice inside you may say, "What would happen if you did?" The generalization statement about women includes an implied modal operator: "Women should not be senior level." Here is a double glitch in the thinking process, a "should not" and a generalization in the same statement. This distorts reality deeply.

If you choose to deal with the generalization, then you simply ask, with a rising inflection of tone, "Never?"

An unspecified "they" often indicates a generalization, as in "They say secretaries cannot wear slacks to work," or "They say his assistants never last long." Finding out who "they" are or checking out the generalization itself can be equally illuminating. "They" may be the coffee vendor who took over the route last week.

Use Pointer 4 on all, every, always, never, they say, everybody, everyone.

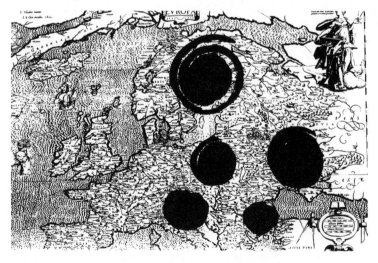

Pointers clarify holes in maps of reality.

The learning process for the little finger is:

LEFT HAND	RIGHT HAND		SEE ON FINGER
SAY TO YOURSELF	ACTION	SAY	SEE ON FINGER
"All"	Lift finger "All?"		Imaginary word *All*
"Always"	Lift finger "Always?"		Imaginary word *Always*
"Everybody"	Lift finger "Everybody?"		Imaginary word *Everybody*
"Never"	Lift finger "Never?"		Imaginary word *Never*
"They"	Lift finger "They? Who are 'they'?"		Imaginary word *They*

POINTER 5: COMPARATORS

Use Pointer 5 on comparators (e.g., better, easier) without antecedents.

The fifth and last Pointer is used for comparators without specific antecedents, such as better, worse, easier, and so on. This Pointer is not quite as useful as the other four, but at times it uncovers useful information. Remember to use a Pointer only when the unexpressed information affects your own or the other's outcome. If you hear, "It's better to do this," you may want to ask, "Better than what?" as long as that question will elicit information you need. Often an unspecific comparator indicates a glitch in the thinking process. On the other hand, you may not need to deal with the glitch.

Another common sentence that could use the fifth Pointer is, "He's the best man for the job." You could ask, "The best man of which group of men?" or you may choose to let this pass. Some people think the best man for a job is a woman.

Your left thumb will recognize a comparator without an antecedent, such as better. Then your right thumb will remember to nudge you into asking "Better than what?" Find the charts, position your hands, and then imagine the word better printed on your left thumb, and the response printed on your right thumb. Use the same learning process as for the other fingers. As soon as you do, your body will have this information and you can use your conscious mind for other matters.

The Pointers' recommended use is as responses to words that are important to your outcome, or to another's outcome in which you are involved. If the meaning of the words does not matter to you, do not whip out your Pointers. Save them for words that matter to your outcome. When you see a fat, abstract word that matters, you definitely need a Pointer. Sometimes even lean, concrete words will need Pointers. Whether the word is specific or needs more clarification depends on the context.

Anytime you are dovetailing outcomes, you need to know the meaning of the other person's nouns and verbs. After you have distinct meanings for the nouns in your communication, then use the second Pointer to find out the exact meaning of any verbs that are important to your outcome.

Before leaving the Pointers, let us look at a historical tragedy that could have been avoided by a single Pointer.

Find out the specific meaning of the nouns first. This will save you the most time.

"Forward, the Light Brigade!"
Was there a man dismay'd?
Not tho' the soldier knew
Someone had blunder'd.
Theirs not to make reply,
Theirs not to reason why,
Theirs but to do and die.
. . .
Into the jaws of death
Into the mouth of hell
Rode the six hundred.
    Alfred, Lord Tennyson
    in *Charge of the Light Brigade*

I was curious about the real message that caused this military blunder. A little research turned up the actual message sent. The ambiguity of the message plus the total situation indicated the need for one Pointer, which, if asked, could have changed the entire battle.

THE MESSAGE	THE POINTER
Lord Raglan wishes the cavalry to advance rapidly to the front.	Which front, specifically?
Follow the enemy. Try to prevent the enemy from carrying away the guns.	
Troop Horse artillery may accompany.	
French cavalry is on your left. Immediate.	

While most of this message is ambiguous, the crux of the ambiguity was "the front." "Which front, specifically?" was the only Pointer needed to save the lives of the 478 soldiers who died. Lord Raglan was on a hill overlooking the battle and knew the positions of his men and the Russians. The Russians were on three sides, so there was not one front, but three. In the heat of battle, Raglan did not realize that those below did not know where the enemy was. His outcome was to capture the Russian guns up the hill, but his nonspecific words sent the Light Brigade off in the wrong direction.

Anyone about to attend a battle—or a meeting—needs the five Pointers to survive and win. While business mis-communication may not send people to their deaths, a lot of hopes, dreams, and outcomes do die there. Now that you have all five Pointers at your fingertips, you have the latest and most portable linguistic tools available for un-wrapping words to discover other people's meanings. The avalanche of words in meetings will hold no terrors for you now that you have added the Pointers to your in-ventory of skills for outcomes, rapport, representational systems, and sensory acuity.

If you think of each person as speaking a mysterious language that sounds like yours but means something different, you take a giant step forward in communication. Once I read about a child who grew up in a Swiss embassy whose staff spoke many different languages. For a long time, the child thought each adult had his own language.

The child was right. Each of us has an individual language, based on our own experiences. These languages sound the same, but the meanings we have given to the sounds are different. Our past experiences color the meanings of our words to such an extent that misunderstandings are common. Misunderstandings are a continuing concern of business because of the time and money they cost. Have you ever explained a project to a subordinate or a peer, only to discover a few weeks later that s/he was working from a totally different idea of the project than yours? Most of us have had this happen more than once. Understanding what others mean by the words they use can save time, effort, and money. The Pointers were created to increase understanding by uncovering useful information about other people's thinking processes. You may suddenly find language more engaging, more of a challenge, and more useful than you would have believed possible.

You are now ready to plan a meeting that succeeds.

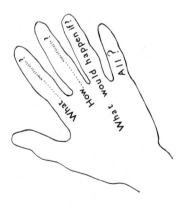

"It goes *THIS* way, stupid!"

*Gahan Wilson,
originally appeared in*
**the Magazine of
Fantasy and Science
Fiction.**

6
Meeting Procedures

Business meetings are like untamed beasts that eat time. Minutes and hours are devoured, chewed up, gone. Discussions, recommendations, conflicts, resolutions, agenda setting, prioritizing, and future planning are necessary, but business people generally agree that meetings could be shorter and more productive.

Some corporations attempt to control meeting time by limiting their time spans, or by holding stand-up meetings or monthly meetings. These solutions have had limited success. None of them addresses the real goal of meetings: group communication for an outcome. Limiting your meeting time is like trying to win a basketball game by shortening the game.

PEGASUS

"Wait a minute," you may say, "my meetings aren't all that bad. I've acquired some useful skills in directing meetings." No doubt, as a successful business person, you do have some meeting skills. My outcome is to make those skills even more effective by adding PEGASUS. An acronym for the seven syntonic meeting procedures, PEGASUS is useful whether you are calling a meeting of two or two hundred people: you and your spouse can decide in less time and with more enjoyment where to go on vacation; your board of directors and stockholders can decide on company policies. PEGASUS lends its wings to your meetings for successful outcomes.

Many business meetings do not succeed. For seven years, four attorneys met together over breakfast from 7:15 to 8:15 a.m. They were supposed to set policies, review procedures, hire additional attorneys and para-legals, assign priorities, and make recommendations to the manager of their law offices. For seven years, they discussed and complained about the law firm's policies. Not once did they make a concerted move to change anything or even go on record as disapproving any issues. The group would not make

RAPPORT

decisions. Their meeting outcome was talk and complaints, though they were not aware of this. Their behaviors reflected their outcome. Behavior is high quality information. If the attorneys had known this was their meetings' outcome, they could have stayed home for breakfast and complained to their spouses.

We have all sat through disastrous meetings, but what can be done? The PEGASUS meeting procedures are designed to answer this question. I personally guarantee them. If you are not successful when you use these procedures in meetings, write me, return the book, and I will personally refund its price.

You already know the most difficult and complex skill for reducing your meeting time and improving the quality of your outcomes: the ability to change goals into an outcome. This employs the five outcome tools:

A. Aim for a specific result
B. Be positive
C. See/hear/feel sensory data
D. Dovetail desires
E. Entertain short- and long-term objectives.

Along with the outcome skills, you need the ability to establish rapport, recognize representational systems, see and hear proficiently, and use the five Pointers. Finally, this chapter will add other tools designed specifically for meetings.

There are three things to do before you call a meeting. First, decide on your outcome. Second, decide on how you will know when you get it (in see/hear/feel data). Third, decide who will attend the meeting.

The attendance list is important. The "two-thirds rule" states that each person invited to the meeting must have information needed for a decision on two out of three agenda items. If there are nine items on the agenda, each person summoned to the meeting should be involved with at least six of the nine agenda items. (If one person is needed for only two of the nine items, you may wish to hold another meeting with a different group for those two items.) This is not a hard and fast rule, but a

Pre-Meeting checklist:

1. Outcome
2. Evidence
3. Two-thirds rule

guideline. Check out different percentages for your meetings and decide what works best for you. If you keep the attendance to those who are necessary and useful, you will cut down talk and time.

The environment—the room, table, chairs, lighting, temperature, and so forth—is also important for the success of the meeting. You should be able to decide the optimum environment for what you want to attain. (I like the story about the businessman who prepared for his IRS audit by transferring all his files into cardboard boxes and not bathing for three days. He is a jogger, and the audit was short. Most of his cardboard boxes were not opened.) Trusting you to arrange the environment, we will proceed to the process of the meeting.

Remember that process focuses on the *how* of doing something. As Michael Doyle and David Straus say in *How to Make Meetings Work*, if you are chewing gum, the chewing is the process and the gum is the content.* These procedures are the recommended processes for any meeting, with any content, with any number of people.

So the day dawns of the first meeting in which you will use the syntonic procedures. If possible, be the first person in the meeting room. This gives you the opportunity to meet each person as s/he enters and check to see if,

* New York: Jove Publications, 1976, p. 25.

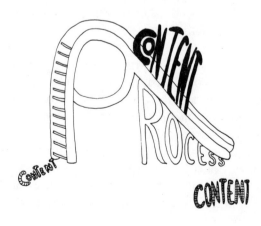

Content and process

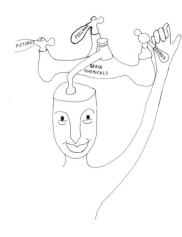

indeed, each is present with all his or her available resources. As you know, just because the person's body is present does not necessarily mean that s/he will be of any use in a meeting. Suppose, as Jim was leaving for the meeting, his major account phoned to cancel a year's contract. This crisis will absorb most of Jim's conscious mind and a certain part of his unconscious mind. Jim may not be useful for the meeting at this time.

You want your staff in a state of high resourcefulness. How can you ensure this? The first step is to recognize whether they are in an optimum state. If you have trained yourself to recognize each staff member's facial expressions and body postures, you will know when anyone is not in a focused state of high resourcefulness at the beginning of the gathering. A few specific questions such as, "What's going on? Are you distracted?" may elicit the information that this person should be elsewhere. If so, depending on the situation, you may want to excuse the individual. Or have a short meeting so s/he can go on. A successful meeting depends on each person being involved and present in mind and body.

Alert relaxation for a resource state of flexibility

As you take the first greeting moments to determine the state of each person, you will also be establishing rapport. Rapport is another reason to meet each person as s/he arrives.

Rapport established, it is time for PEGASUS. The seven procedures to keep your meeting on the right trajectory and to reach your outcomes are:

P. Present outcomes

E. Explain evidence

G. Gain agreement on outcomes

A. Activate sensory acuity

S. Summarize each major decision

U. Use the relevancy challenge

S. Summarize the next step (at end of meeting)

RAPPORT

Present Outcomes

The best way to present your desired outcome or outcomes of the meeting is to write them down so that each member has a visible reminder of why s/he is in the meeting. A blackboard or a flip-chart is useful for displaying the written outcome. The outcome sets the boundaries for all discussion and keeps the participants focused.

Explain Evidence

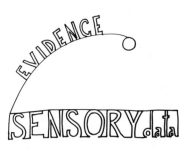

The evidence procedure tells participants the criteria for a successful meeting. How will they know the meeting is a success? What will they see, hear, and feel as evidence of achieving the outcome?

The Chief Executive Officer might present his outcome and evidence this way: "This meeting is to discuss the manufacture and sales picture for the six new pieces of software for 1983. I'll know we've been successful if we set up the budget requirements for both manufacturing and sales, determine the time frame for the first 4000 units, and decide whether new personnel are needed to satisfy the time allotted." On the flip chart, he writes:

BUDGET
MANUFACTURING
SALES
TIME—4,000 UNITS
PERSONNEL?

In this example, establishing the budget, the time frame, and the decision about personnel would be the evidence that the meeting was successfully completed:

BUDGET: $750,000
MANUFACTURING: 500,000
SALES: 250,000
TIME—4000 UNITS: 3 Months
PERSONNEL: Yes

At the end, everyone can see the budget figures, the time alloted, and the yes or no on additional personnel. They can hear the agreements and feel satisfied with the decisions. At this point, the meeting will be a success. Meanwhile, there are other interim steps.

Gain Agreement on Outcomes

This step is crucial to the effectiveness of the meeting procedures. Check with each person in the meeting, one at a time, to see that s/he does indeed agree on the stated outcomes. This agreement can be verified with a look and confirmed by a verbal response from each person. You need a complete visual and auditory confirmation that each member agrees on these outcomes.

Once you have an agreement on outcomes, then you can keep the meeting moving in the direction you wish. Side trips into irrelevancy eat up time. If the outcome is clear to all, and each person has publicly agreed to support information and solutions leading to that outcome, then all other issues become irrelevant and can be cut off quickly. This includes hidden agendas—goals desired by one or more participants but which oppose the outcome of the meeting.

If anyone disputes the outcome, sort this out at the beginning. Unless participants agree about the destination, you may end up in Toronto when you meant to go to Miami. To spot any disagreement or hidden agenda holdout during this Gain Agreement procedure, you will need your sensory acuity.

> If each person publicly agrees to support the outcome, then all other issues and hidden agendas become irrelevant and are easily quashed.

Activate Sensory Acuity

Sensory acuity is useful everywhere, but especially in the vortex of a meeting. Sensory awareness needs to be used with each procedure to see and hear the procedures are working as desired.

Use sensory acuity for spotting incongruency. Congruence was defined earlier as agreement of all parts of the personality. Incongruency is disagreement of one or more parts of the personality. Incongruencies often show up when someone has a hidden agenda.

Sensory acuity will make you aware of incongruities of others. Incongruencies cancel out verbal agreements on outcomes. Incongruency is present when a member's mouth is saying "yes" and his/her head is shaking "no." If his pencil is moving back and forth, right to left,

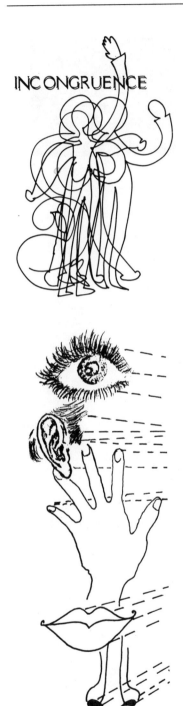

INCONGRUENCE

this may be a "no" signal as well, even if he is nodding his head "yes." If her mouth is smiling but her eyes are steely, this may be an incongruity—or not.

Incongruencies may need exploring—or not. The timing for exploring incongruencies should be selected by you, since you are running the meeting. When you notice a sign of incongruence, you may want to make a mental note with a question mark. Then you can be alert to other sensory feedback later, or you may want to confront it right away. The entire situation will indicate your best choice of behavior. Sometimes the best way to handle a hidden agenda is to make it irrelevant to the outcome. Sometimes a confrontation is in order. If you are in control of the processes of the meeting, you make this choice.

If the incongruence is because of a hidden agenda, this other agenda will probably appear at some point. You may be able to deal with the hidden agenda by the use of several different procedures as the meeting progresses. You may elect to deal with the incongruency directly, now, by saying something such as, "You seem to have some hesitancy about accepting this outcome. Did you have something else in mind for this meeting?"

The answer will indicate to you where to go next in view of your outcomes.

Summarize Each Major Decision

If you summarize each major decision as you proceed, participants know where they are and where they have been and can compare this with the meeting's outcome.

The words you select for the backtrack can be influencing mechanisms. As psychologist George A. Miller said, "The most powerful stimulus for changing minds is not a chemical. Or a baseball bat. It is a word."[*] By choosing words that are congruent with the outcomes and representational systems of the people at the meeting, you

* George A. Miller, interviewed by Elizabeth Hall in "Giving Away Psychology in the '80s," *Psychology Today,* January 1980, p. 41.

will be able to focus on and gain agreement about those outcomes.

Check the responses of the group with each summary. Notice congruent agreement, slight disagreement, and incongruencies. Ascertain any opposition or signs of a storm brewing. This awareness of potential opposition and where it lies, and educated guesses about solutions will give you a useful edge. If you need to confront and accommodate disagreement, you will have time to get ready.

Here is an example of one CEO's mini-outcome summary. "James is concerned about the number of faulty generators in Model 7118. We've sold 3,456 of these this year, and 247 have been returned for repairs. This number concerns me as well. We're here to determine the original cause of the breakdowns and to decide what can be done now.

"We've agreed on probable causes. First, the Number 12 machine seems to have been the cause. This machine has already been repaired. Then we agreed on four new checking procedures. This is the present situation. Now let's decide how best to repair the returned generators."

During this summary, the CEO would be checking agreement, congruence, incongruence, and disagreement in facial and body responses of the participants.

Use the Relevancy Challenge

The relevancy challenge is the question: *How is this relevant?* The challenge is effective only when appropriate and if all the earlier steps about outcome agreement have been accomplished. If you use the relevancy question consistently, each participant will quickly realize what information is relevant and what is off base.

Challenge the information, not the person.

The relevancy challenge has many psychological uses. A simple question, it can be used with great politeness or extreme irascibility, depending on the situation. If the person proposing information is able to establish its relevance, then the information is allowed. If the relevance is not clear, the information is cut off. This keeps the meeting on target.

The secret is to challenge not the person, only his or her information. Then you cannot be accused of favoritism. Your decisions appear impersonal and based on relevancy alone. In a short time, the relevancy challenge becomes like a teacher's ruler: it reminds the members of the meeting to make their own relevancy check before they open their mouths. Since the relevancy challenge has disciplinary overtones, you must remember to maintain rapport.

At the same time, if one or two members are slow in learning to produce only relevant information, you may become more and more stern as you pose the relevancy challenge. As meetings become shorter and more productive, participants come to appreciate the relevancy challenge.

You may choose to point to the written outcome when you ask the relevancy question. After two or three times, pointing to the written outcome is all that is needed to ask for relevancy. This nonverbal stimulus-response mechanism is extremely powerful and speeds up the training for relevancy.

The relevancy challenge is the appropriate response for any proposal based on a hidden agenda. If the proposal is not relevant, it is not allowed. Simply pointing to the written outcome will quickly kill off hidden agendas and any other irrelevant proposals. Once the irrelevancies are cut out, outcomes are easier to attain.

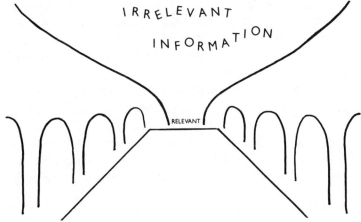

Summarize the Next Step

You have achieved your outcomes. The meeting is almost complete. First, though, you need to summarize the meeting's major decisions, the final outcome, and the next step to be made by the group or by individuals. In some cases, assign specific dates for those next steps.

Next step

Some fine-tuning occurs as you use these PEGASUS procedures. Keep in mind that once you have presented your outcome to the group, it may be apparent that some information needed for this outcome is not available at the moment. Adjourn the meeting until a time when this information is available. You did not attain your original outcome, but you can consider the meeting to be a success in that you went as far as possible and adjourned without wasting time.

In some meetings, you have to change outcomes. Being aware of this is a powerful asset in itself. Ted Graske, an executive with American Express, told me about being sent to a meeting in Denver to explain the proper procedures for prompt payment of expense accounts. Within half an hour, he became aware that the fifteen people present were full of resentments about expense accounts and could not concentrate on the new procedures. He whipped off the flip-chart page with his outcome and wrote "Complaints to Home Office about Expense Account Policy." He then conducted the meeting with the new outcome. The meeting was successful in that he acquired lots of complaints. Employee morale is actually more important to AMEX than procedures, as Ted knew. A few weeks later, he returned to Denver to carry out the original assignment and found the employees much more receptive.

I taught these PEGASUS procedures to a computer operator at a library research corporation. Within a month she was covertly keeping the company's meeting time to a minimum and producing quality outcomes. Within two months, the president would look toward her if someone got off the subject. She would politely issue the relevancy challenge. If you are running the meeting, the skills of outcome setting, rapport, and pointers are all you need besides PEGASUS (which includes sensory acuity and the relevancy challenge). However, to steal a meeting you need some extra skills.

HOW TO TAKE OVER A MEETING

First of all, to take over a meeting from someone else means taking a risk. How big a risk depends on many factors, but you need to be sure the potential gain is worth the risk. Do some downside planning. What is the worst thing that could happen? If you decide to go ahead, here are guidelines.

If you decide to take over a meeting that has been called by someone else, there are several ways to do this, some riskier than others. Among the following possibilities, you may find one that suits your needs.

- You might say, "I'm lost. Why are we here?" and look at the manager in charge of the meeting. This may elicit an outcome. You can base any relevancy challenges on that outcome.
- You can escalate the irrelevant discussions until someone else brings the group back to the goal or topic. If the meeting was called to fix the price of a yard of sand, and you are talking about your children dripping sand all over your new rug, someone else may get the meeting back on target. Then you can ask, "What specifically are we trying to accomplish?"

- If there is so much irrelevancy and such a fuzzy goal that you despair, you can stand up, turn over your chair abruptly, move somewhere else, and calmly ask, "Is the outcome of this meeting to [define your best outcome]?" Your behavior will interrupt everyone's train of thought and their expectations. This is called a *pattern interruption.* It is as if you have stopped their tapes or pulled their plugs. For a moment, they will be susceptible to your suggestion. They will be surprised, confused, and uncomfortable enough to want a way out. If you offer an acceptable suggestion for their thoughts to follow, they will probably agree. Keep their outcomes in mind, or this will not work. Do not explain the overturned chair or the move, simply go on as if nothing untoward had occurred.

*Pattern-interrupts pull
the plug.*

- A computer engineer told me about this variation on pattern interruption. Two department heads were in conflict in a meeting. They yelled at each other, made accusations and denials, etc., but were accomplishing nothing. The engineer quietly got up and left. This was a pattern interruption, but without a suggestion on his part as to what to do next. Although pattern interruptions are most effective when you stay around to make a suggestion, this exit worked for the engineer's outcome. The two department heads called another meeting for later. In the meantime, each came to him and apologized for his behavior. The next meeting went smoothly.
- If you are fed up with the meeting's procedures, chaos, and irrelevancies, you might look at your watch and announce loudly, "I have five more minutes for this meeting. What had you hoped to accomplish?"
- You can offer to conduct a meeting for someone else when they are extremely busy or out of town. Use the meeting to demonstrate the procedures to others who may then help you keep future meetings on track
- Model good meeting behavior. If you act out the procedures in the portions of the meeting under your control—say, when you give a departmental report—then people will begin to learn from you. This is somewhat slow but effective. It is difficult to continue to be unproductive when productive behavior is being demonstrated in front of you. Some people can resist learning , however.
- You can provide the summary or backtrack and use this procedure to maintain a trajectory you want.

Two more points are useful for fine-tuning meetings. First, a successful meeting needs a fine balance between structure and freedom. The PEGASUS procedures are designed to gain your outcomes in the shortest possible time. You also need a small amount of freedom from structure to promote creativity. Once the procedures are accepted, meetings will proceed toward outcomes at a fast pace. You may want to include some time and space for brainstorming or playing with future possibilities or for the creative free flow of ideas. The balance between freedom and structure can shift through time but should be kept in mind.

Once PEGASUS has become an accepted part of your meetings, your staff will begin to look forward to attending. They will know when they have relevant information to contribute, what they have accomplished in the meeting, and how to proceed next.

Syntonics—a new discipline which has evolved from several older disciplines. See chart on pg. 127

PEGASUS makes for relevancy

Syntonics Theory

ORGANIZATION and NEW INSIGHTS: ....John Grinder and Richard Bandler

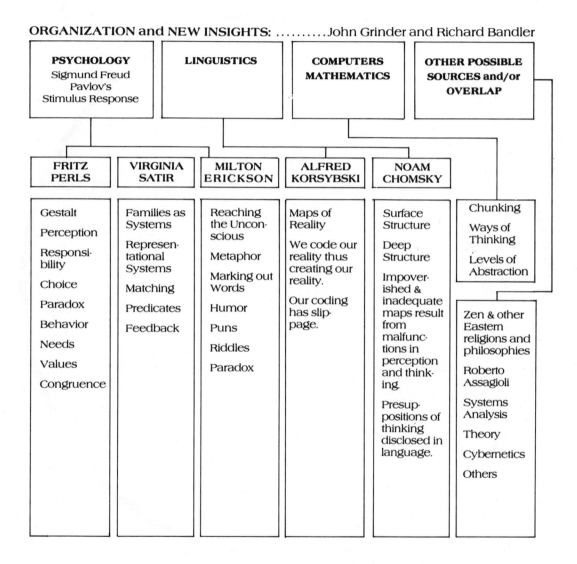

PSYCHOLOGY Sigmund Freud Pavlov's Stimulus Response	**LINGUISTICS**	**COMPUTERS MATHEMATICS**	**OTHER POSSIBLE SOURCES and/or OVERLAP**

FRITZ PERLS	**VIRGINIA SATIR**	**MILTON ERICKSON**	**ALFRED KORSYBSKI**	**NOAM CHOMSKY**	
Gestalt Perception Responsi- bility Choice Paradox Behavior Needs Values Congruence	Families as Systems Represen- tational Systems Matching Predicates Feedback	Reaching the Uncon- scious Metaphor Marking out Words Humor Puns Riddles Paradox	Maps of Reality We code our reality thus creating our reality. Our coding has slip- page.	Surface Structure Deep Structure Impover- ished & inadequate maps result from malfunc- tions in perception and think- ing. Presup- positions of thinking disclosed in language.	Chunking Ways of Thinking Levels of Abstraction Zen & other Eastern religions and philosophies Roberto Assagioli Systems Analysis Theory Cybernetics Others

ADDITIONAL APPLICATIONS: .... Judith DeLozier, Leslie Cameron-Bandler,
Robert Bilts, David Gordon, Lynne Conwell,
Michael LeBeau, Norma and Phil Barreta.

SYNTONICS for BUSINESS COMMUNICATION:...... LEFT BRAIN ORGANIZATION, Robert Hill

SYNTONICS for BUSINESS COMMUNICATION: ....**Emphasis** on INTEGRITY and RIGHT
BRAIN ORGANIZATION Genie Z. Laborde

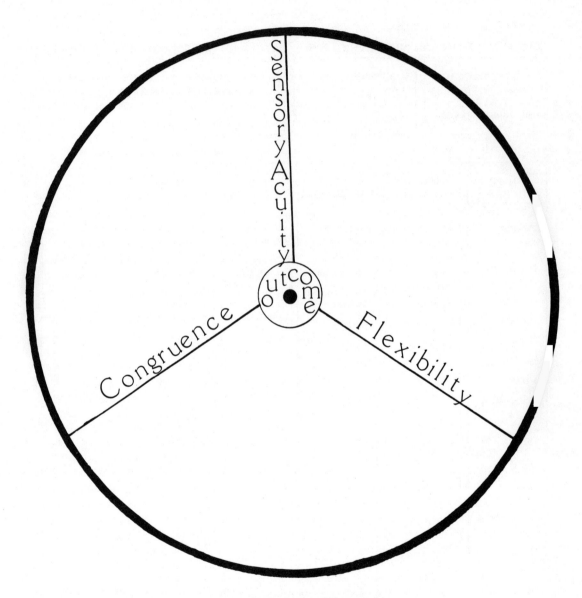

Sensory Acuity

Outcome

Congruence

Flexibility

If what you're doing is not working, forget the content and check these.

7
Flexibility

Now that you know how to set an outcome, establish rapport, use sensory acuity, and use the Pointers, the time has come to look at the intricacies of behavior, especially where behavior affects communication. Behavior is a significant piece of the communication process. If you tell your employer you are dedicated to your company and arrive for work late each morning, which counts more, your words or your behavior? Has anyone ever said one thing to you and done the opposite? Which counts more, words or behavior?

The highest quality information in communication is behavioral. Witherspoon, Birdwhistell, Mehrabian, Bandler, and Grinder are linguists who take the position that nonverbal responses usually are more significant than the words in the communication process.

Communication includes the total behaviors of the two or more people in the communication process. Communication is also the patterns of the behaviors: the repetitions, the rhythms, the variations, and the polarity shifts occurring in the interaction.

In communication neither person acts in a vacuum. Feedback and feed-forward processes occur constantly. Each action, behavior, and word affects the other person. The interaction between people is the mysterious and ambiguous part of the communication process. It is as if the most important part of communication happens in the middle, where the behaviors and words of one person meet the behaviors and words of the other and change in the meeting. Noticing how your words change meaning in this middle zone is the key to good communication.

What is going on inside the other person? Is s/he understanding you, or does s/he indeed have a different meaning for your words? Often we find when we thought we had agreement on meanings, our subsequent behaviors indicate that we were not in agreement. We were deeply involved in miscommunication.

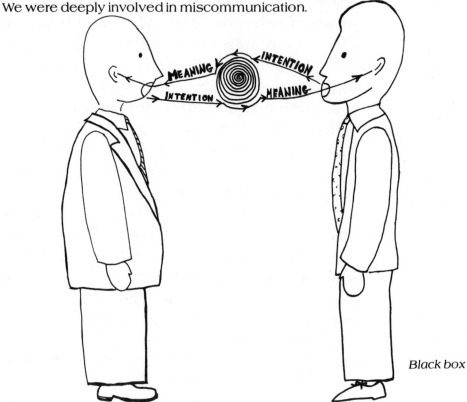

Black box

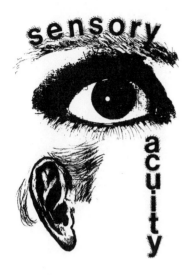

The meaning of any communication is the response.

Feedback loop

If you are not getting the response you want, take a different tack. Be flexible.

MEANING IS RESPONSE/BEHAVIOR

You decide your intention, but whether you succeed in communication depends on transferring your intention to the other person. The other person decides the meaning. You can detect whether your message has been received correctly if you use sensory acuity. You can be alert to signs that your intention has gone astray and that you must do or say something else.

Being able to change your approach is the subject of this chapter. Even when they recognize miscommunication, some people never change. They just keep doing the same thing—only louder. We all know intuitively that behaviors do communicate louder than words. Yet we often overlook important behaviors that are telling us clearly what is going on in the other person's perception and thinking. By now you should be able to use your sensory acuity to discern what the other person thinks you mean. Next, you can vary your behavior to get the response you want.

Flexibility means having choices in the communication interaction. In *Frogs into Princes*, Bandler and Grinder point out that if you have only one choice in responding, you are a robot. If you have two choices, you have a dilemma. If you have three choices, you have flexibility. Five choices are even better. If you are flexible enough, you can correct your behavior to elicit the responses you want. If you only have one set of responses to any one signal, you will not be able to change your behavior when it does not produce the results you want.

Communication is a circular feedback system in which responses elicit responses. Behaviors elicit behaviors. Words elicit words. Flexibility means you can use the information uncovered by this feedback system. Communicating with flexibility is like navigating an airplane. Unless airplanes are equipped with expensive navigational aids, they still fly a zigzag path, being constantly corrected by the pilots in response to radio signals. Knowing this helps the conversational pilot, who needs to correct his or her responses to the signals of

the other person in the conversation. A zigzag approach, with corrections, is often the shortest route to your outcome.

Flexibility in setting outcomes is another important piece of the communication process. Have you known anyone who had a goal not worth having? Who continued toward the goal even when evidence piled up that the goal was garbage? This is only one example of inflexibility.

Being flexible means being responsive to change and being adaptable. In the communication process you can have flexibility in words, in thinking, in perception, and in behaviors. The Pointers encourage flexibility in words. Sensory acuity encourages flexibility in perception. This chapter is concerned, for the most part, with flexibility in behaviors. Flexible behaviors are the "open sesame" to blocked outcomes.

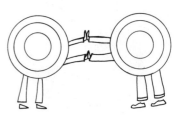

UNCOMPLICATING FLEXIBILITY

If flexibility is such a good idea, why are most of us inflexible? Especially, why are we not flexible when once we were?

Young children, by and large, are flexible. Take a toy away from a child and s/he will play with his or her toes

Polarity Response

Polarity shifts: Going from Yes to No or Black to white.

or the car keys or a piece of string. Children usually lose this flexibility as they grow up. Three natural parts of the growing-up process seem to interfere with flexibility. Increasing your awareness of these natural propensities can improve your flexibility.

1. *We like to be liked.* While growing up, as we interact with family and friends, we learn that certain behaviors elicit approval from others. We tend to repeat those behaviors, which ultimately become habits. At one time these habitual behaviors got us what we wanted—approval—and we tend to fall back on them. When these behaviors no longer get us what we want, we feel disappointed but do not know how to change.

2. *We enjoy our polarity responses.* At age two and again during the teen years, we begin to explore what it is like *not* to do what family and friends want and expect us to do. We know what they want, and we do the opposite. We explore disapproval, and some of us get stuck in these polarity responses. We become so accustomed to doing the opposite of the expected that we ignore our own inflexibility. Having to have a polarity response is as limiting as having to have approval.

3. *We think we are our behavior.* This third phenomenon follows from the first two and is the most destructive to flexibility. Flexibility is easy once you unlearn this fallacy. You and your behavior are not one and the same. If you were, then when you did something dumb, *you* would be dumb. Then again, when you did something intelligent, you would be intellligent. Now how can you be both dumb and intelligent?

You and I are not both dumb and smart, but we can *act* in both ways. We are not our actions. This seems obvious, but lots of people identify with their behaviors so closely that they cannot recognize dumb behavior in themselves. They feel that if they admit their behavior was dumb, then they would *be* dumb. Actually, it is sometimes a relief to admit, "Well, that was a dumb move, but I can learn from it." Once you separate yourself from your behaviors, at least slightly, you have many more choices.

I like to think of my behaviors as reflecting me at a moment in time. Behaviors are like clothes I can put on or take off. Sometimes I outgrow clothes, and sometimes my taste in clothes changes. Things that used to fit no longer do. The same is true for behaviors. Just as my clothes reflect me at this moment in time, so do my behaviors.

When I change, my behaviors can change, too. I have heard a lot of intelligent people say in response to well-made suggestions from others, "Oh, I couldn't do that. That wouldn't be me." Of course *that* wouldn't be you. *That* would only be a new behavior you were trying out to see if it fit better than some old behavior.

We are not our behaviors. We are responsible for our behaviors, but our behaviors are not us.

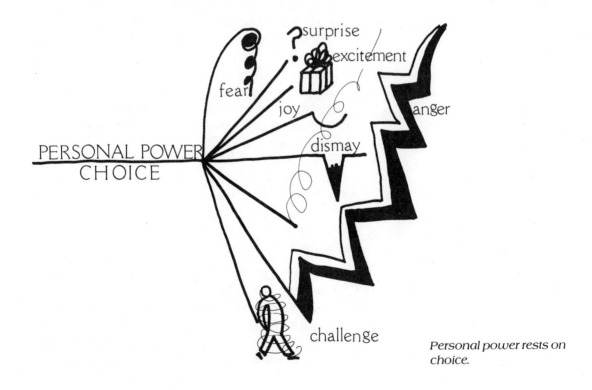

Personal power rests on choice.

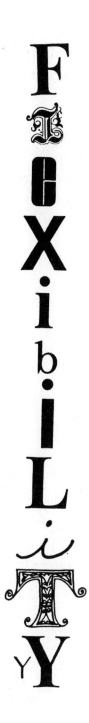

Old behaviors have the comfort of being familiar. Even when they are not successful in helping us gain our present outcomes, they are as comfortable as an old set of clothes. Trying on new behaviors is a risk. Who knows what will happen?

Exactly. No one knows what will happen, except that the response from other people will be different. This, of course, is the best reason to try out new behaviors—to elicit new responses from others until you elicit the response you want.

I am not talking about breaking the law or going against your own integrity. I am talking about simple behavior changes, such as kissing your wife before she kisses you. You would be surprised at the things people cannot bring themselves to do. As one bored, depressed housewife and no-longer-needed mother told me, "I couldn't go out and get a job. Who would do the dishes? I'm a homemaker. Homemakers stay at home."

This poor woman had identified herself as a homemaker. In her world view, homemakers have and do not have certain behaviors. If she got a job, who would she be? Somebody else. She was caught on a vicious track, a stimulus-response that was ruining her marriage and her life.

Disadvantages of Flexibility

Flexibility does have drawbacks. These are not necessarily horrible consequences but you may want to be forewarned.

1. Friends and family will pressure you to remain the same. It may make them uncomfortable to see you change.
2. It is easier to follow your habitual behavior.
3. You may have an identity crisis. Who am I? If I am not my behavior, who am I? You are the one who chooses what behaviors you wish. You may know you are not your behavior, but you may believe

your behaviors should be consistent, not contradictory. (Consistency resembles rigor mortis, you know.)

4. You may surprise yourself.

Advantages of Flexibility

1. You are more able to elicit the responses you want. If what you are doing is not getting the response you want, you can do something else that will. And something else. The entire point of being flexible in behavior is that you can change your behaviors until you get the response you want.

2. You can utilize your behaviors to change other people. Our behaviors are not us, but our behaviors do affect those around us. We might consider changing our behaviors at least as often as we change clothes. Checking your behavior closet and adding a few new styles could lead to extraordinary changes. Human beings have a tendency to do the same thing once the stimulus-response has become set. Doing the same thing will keep getting the same response. When you change your behavior, the usual response of someone else changes, too.

    Let's look at an example. A client asked for a new behavior to use when her boss yelled at her. Usually she got angry or cried. I suggested she imagine herself walking on the beach; in the distance, this angry man was "acting out." This allowed her to stay calm.

    Since it takes two to argue, if one switches a response anywhere in the pattern, the other has to switch, too, or be stuck in an incongruent response. The one who first breaks out of a negative or damaging pattern which is not leading to his outcome is the one exercising personal power.

3. You will increase your personal power. Some people feel it is not authentic to respond in any way except with the first emotion that surfaces. Considering several different emotions will give you a choice. (Is the second or third less authentic or less

Stimulus-response is the way we learn

The Stimulus-Response function of the brain creates habits

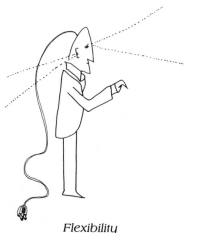

Flexibility

honest than the first?) The potential for more powerful responses lies in increased choices. Perhaps the second or third choice will be more useful in gaining your outcome. If your outcome is authentic, perhaps it is wiser to choose from several authentic responses, rather than to respond like an authentic robot.

4. You can discover talents, propensities, attractions, and passions you would not have known in your old rut of stimulus-response.
5. People will be attracted to your many-sided personality.
6. Life will be an adventure.

How do you make flexibility a part of your life? Flexibility is like any other skill. You have to practice to be good at it. The best way to practice is to interrupt your habits and do something different. Since the body and the mind are not separate, you will find you can increase your mental flexibility by loosening up your body. All the muscles of your body have learned your old patterns of responding. Not only your brain learns to be afraid, but also your shoulders and your stomach. Your mouth knows the fear response as well. Change these rigid, frozen muscles and you will find yourself responding with more flexibility.

Many disciplines work for a flexible body, including massage, Rolfing, exercise, jogging, yoga, T'ai Chi, Arica, ballet, Jazzercise, and Feldenkrais. All of these are useful for changing muscle patterns.

Flexible body, flexible mind.

shoulds

OK, so you are convinced that flexibility in communication is a good idea. How do you get it?

Here are specific steps.

- Interrupt old patterns—drive to work a different way, for instance.
- When you notice you are acting inside a "should," change role models for three minutes. Be somebody else.
- Switch channels of perception.

- Switch sequences of information when making a decision.
- When you find you are successful in what you are doing, do it differently. Try something new. Success can stop you from learning flexibility. If you usually consult pictures, then sounds, and then feelings, concentrate on reversing the order. (Easier said than done.)
- In low-risk situations, stop what you are doing and think of three alternate routes to your outcome.
- Do not listen to content of communication for one minute. Watch only, or listen to tone only. Decide what you *know* about the other person that you would not know from the content.
- Pretend there are no secrets. Our unconscious minds perceive, compute, and store so much information that we know more about other people than we realize or admit.
- All of us are doing the best we can, knowing what we know and given our life experiences at each moment. Select the behavior on your part that will elicit the optimum behavior on the part of another.
- For one day, leave everyone you interact with in any way in a better state than when you found them. (Would you like to try for two days?)
- Do something you have never done before: write poetry, learn scuba diving, do yoga, have a baby, bleach your hair, pretend you are from another planet for a day.
- Look at the world through a new set of glasses. Pretend you are your next-door neighbor for an hour. How does the world look? Pretend you are 17 or 93 years old.
- Do not talk for one week. Write notes. Inform your family and friends you are doing an experiment. Buckminster Fuller once was silent for one year.
- Match movements of another with minimal movements and notice rapport.

Stimulus-responses are associations set up in the brain

Polarity Response

- Remember a time when you had an argument with someone you loved. You knew you were right. You hurt them in this argument. But you knew you were right. Now, remember the argument in great detail: colors, sounds, time of year, facial expressions. Run the film backward. Then, run it forward. Add appropriate music and run it again. Next, add inappropriate music and run it again. Run the film backward once more. Then, run the film forward. Do you feel any different this time than the first time you watched this memory?

- Make a list of all your habits for a week. The following week, change the time of day you do each habit. Do some of them in different sequences. Notice any difference.

- Pay more attention to smells for one day. Or intensify your own smells: wear cologne more, or less deodorant.

- In the middle of a raucous argument, capitulate. Say, "You're totally right. Now what would you like?" (You do not have to do whatever they say.)

- Find models for flexible behavior. Some of the Marx Brothers films have good models for flexible behaviors. If you need a role model for flexibility, find *Duck Soup* on the late, late show.

- Be flexible in your outcomes.

Stop and make sure the outcome is worth having. If you have to go through a lot of discomfort, is the outcome even possible? Farfetched is OK, feasible is absolutely necessary. Some goals are not worth having. Check your outcomes with see, hear, and feel questions to be sure you would want them once you got them, and that they are worth your effort. If not, being flexible about your outcome is the next move.

Flexibility in outcomes, flexibility in timing, and flexibility in words will increase your effectiveness in communicating. Flexibility in perception, in thinking, and in actions will increase your effectiveness in influencing others. This is especially evident in the area of sales.

8
Syntonic Sales Techniques

Making a sale is a subcategory of negotiating. And the art of salesmanship is selling fantasy. You do not sell an idea or a product, you sell the fantasy of what it will do for its owner. Selling a strategy, for example, means selling success. When you sell insurance, you sell peace of mind. If you are selling lipstick, you are selling beauty. When you sell a washing machine, you sell cleanliness. When you sell a stereo, you sell the pleasure of music. Selling Jacuzzis is selling relaxation. When you sell your boss on an idea, it is just another fantasy, a fantasy that may or may not come true.

Successful salespeople know this. Since the first clay pot was sold by the anticipation of a cool drink without going to the stream, salespeople have focused on the customer's *outcome*. When I teach communication seminars, the salespeople in the audience catch on first. They already know a lot of what I teach.

Many of the syntonic skills for making sales successfully have already been presented. Determining outcomes, gaining rapport, matching representational systems, and using sensory acuity to gauge responses are extremely effective in sales presentations. They are also practically irresistible. so use them with extreme caution.

A boutique's high-pressure salesperson once talked me into buying an expensive dress. I never liked wearing it, I discovered later: my curves turned into bulges in this particular style. I no longer shop at that boutique.

So be sure the customer wants whatever you are selling. The three snakes of Remorse, Recrimination, and Resentment and the dragon of Revenge will eat you alive unless you use these skills with integrity.

You could think of selling as a negotiation, but easier. The client or potential customer is usually neutral rather than opposed. You do not have to move him or her 180 degrees, only 90 degrees. This can usually be done by simply providing information.

> Integrity means dovetailing outcomes.

RESOURCE STATE

The most useful first step a salesperson could take is to move into a resource state. *Resource state* is another

---

Resource States

1. Recall a time when you did something extraordinarily well.
2. Ask yourself, "What did I see?"
   "What did I hear?"
   "What did I feel?"
3. Touch the back of one hand with a finger of the other hand when the memory of the experience peaks in intensity.
4. Test to be sure you have set up a stimulus-response to your own touch. If not, do the four steps again.

name for an optimum internal state of psychological excellence. This state is established in the here and now, but it is based on a memory of a time when you did something extraordinarily well. Jim Banks accessed a resource state in the vignette in chapter 1.

To set up a resource state, all you have to do is ask yourself: What did I see when I did this extraordinary feat?*

What did I hear?

What did I feel?

When the memory with sensory-based data reaches its fullest intensity for you, touch the back of one hand with a finger of the other hand. This creates a stimulus-response association with that spot. You can recall this state of excellence any time, at will, by touching that same spot. Or you can assign a word to the experience, and the word will also call up the memory. Or you can use both touch and an assigned word.

Having a friend who watches you and touches the back of your hand when you are ready works even better for setting up your resource state. Run through the sequence twice to be sure you can touch your hand or say the key word and immediately recall the memory of doing something very well.

Once you have learned how to recall your resource state quickly, you can spend as much time there as you

* Be sure you are looking out at the world through your own eyes, not watching yourself in your mind's eye as though you were outside your own body.

wish. The extraordinary thing is that once you are in a re-source state, the experiences you have acquired during your life are readily available as possible guidelines and resources for action. You can move into the appropriate response to any situation with great ease and rapidity.

Once you have your resource state well in hand, you are in the optimum frame of mind for a sales call. In a sales presentation, as in any communication, rapport is the first order of business. The small talk at the beginning of an interaction can often be all you need for rapport. Small talk can also give you a lot of useful information about sorting principles, time perceptions, what is important, and which representational system the client is using at this time.

If you do not have rapport, do not disclose your out-come. Do not proceed until you have established rap-port. If credibility is missing, find a way to get it so that your rapport skills will work. You are not going anywhere without rapport.

Once you have established rapport, either through mirroring or matching, you can test this rapport by a technique known as *pacing and leading*. In pacing and leading, if one person makes a new move or modifies a current one, the other will follow. This occurs naturally when rapport exists. In fact, it occurs so fast that it is sometimes difficult to tell who is pacing or matching and who is leading.

Rapport becomes a dance in which each person's rhythm is matched by his partner.

This can be useful in sales as long as you are sure the other's outcome in this interaction is compatible with yours. You can determine this by "qualifying" the buyer. During this step, you find out the other's outcome and whether s/he can pay for or use your service, product, or idea; you also set out your own position in the transac-tion, which is one of equal status. You might think of yourself as a trader. You will trade your service, product, or idea for something of less or equal value.

You are also an educator. You are here to teach the customer what is available to satisfy his or her outcome. To do this, you must help articulate their outcomes as early as possible.

UNICORN

The mnemonic device for a sales call is UNICORN.

U. Use Pointers for outcomes
N. Nudge the buyer's see/hear/feel fantasy
I. Implement the As If and future planning techniques
C. Conditional close
O. Outcome dovetailing
R. Rapport
N. Next step and summary

Use Pointers to Clarify Outcomes

The obvious tools to use in finding out the outcome of your customers are the Pointers. Remember the softeners: "I'm curious about what specific needs . . ." etc.

Before the small talk is over, you should be able to ask what *specific* needs his company has that your product, service, or idea will fill. These may not be the words you use. In fact, I recommend that you select words that are familiar to those working in that business. If you are working with grocers, you can talk about fresh produce, repeat customers, fuzzy peaches, and loss leaders. They will know what you mean.

You will gain friends as well as customers as long as you keep your eye on their outcomes and your ears tuned to their vocabulary. If you use words your customers have already used, you know they have a meaning for that word coded on their map. Use your sensory acuity to select words with positive responses attached. This is such a powerful technique that I hesitate to discuss it without mentioning the four Rs. By using another's words, which they have already presented to you on a silver platter by talking, and selecting only words with positive responses, you can sell anybody anything—almost. They will return it on Monday, however, unless it satisfies a need they genuinely have.

Once you know syntonics, the only skill you need for selling is matching a need with a product, service, or

Enter the other person's world with the correct passwords to his reality.

POINTER
HAND

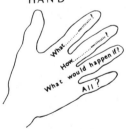

Softeners and pointers

idea. As a syntonics sales person, you are a match-maker. You already know your idea, service, or product is worth having or you would not be selling it. If you spend all your time and energy on matching, you are headed straight for success.

If there is not a match, shake hands and move on. You will save both of you precious time and reap invaluable good will. Leave your card so if the person has a need later, s/he can contact you. S/he will remember you. You will stand out as an extraordinarily competent and responsible individual.

Next, See/Hear/Feel Fantasy

When you discover your customer does have a need you can fill, the see/hear/feel technique comes next. The dynamic way to sell is to walk your client right into his own fantasy and show him what the reality will be like. Then let him listen to the sounds, then get the feeling: "If you actually do agree with me about adding Philadelphia to our eastern territories, then you would see our sales having a 50 percent increase in the next three months and you would hear the chairman of the board say, 'What a good job you've done,' and you would feel good about incorporating this idea into our future planning."

The fantasy about owning your product, enjoying your service, or buying your idea will take over, and you can relax. At that point, you probably have clinched the sale. On the other hand, if the fantasy does not take over, you are wasting your time. Shake hands and move on.

If, As If, and Future Planning

The As If technique is a fantasy so familiar to business people that they do not bridle at its introduction. They have forgotten it is make-believe because they use it all the time. It is an accepted part of their thinking processes. They call the As If process *future planning*. In future planning, even the most unimaginative businessman will pretend that what is happening now will continue, or get better, or get worse; he then works out a business plan with these elements.

Moving on is merely postponing success.

IF YOU GET A FIT
You've got a sale

You can use the As If technique to find out the fantasy outcome of your customer. The sequence of words will go something like this: "As I understand you, you would like to double your volume in the next twelve months. In order to do this you need a [your product, service, or idea] which will [do whatever your product, service, or idea does]. If I can demonstrate that my [product, service, or idea] will do this, we will have a mutually satisfactory agreement."

The only caveat in the use of As If is that you keep your own fantasy and your customer's fantasy within the realm of the reasonable. Do not promise more than you can deliver. The As If is seductive in that words can create castles in the air. Be sure you have the know-how to build the castle before you sign a contract.

The purpose of the As If technique is to discover your customer's outcome. Then you can determine whether you can match outcomes, which is essential to any sale.

Future planning is not a sales technique per se, but it is useful. In future planning, business people figure out their business outcomes for one year, three years, five years, and ten years in the future. To do this, they pretend certain things will happen. Most business people sit in the present, with present figures in front of them, and guess what will happen in five years.

A much better way to plan is to pretend you are sitting in your office five years from now, at the end of five years of success. You look at your successful figures for the past five years and answer the question, "How did we achieve such successful growth?"

Thinking backward is easier and more creative than thinking forward.

This small shift in perspective can produce amazing information. You act as if you are in the future. See, hear, and feel your success. Then look back to find out how you achieved your desired state.

Businesses play around with looking forward in all their future planning sessions, but they usually overlook this small shift. Looking backward triggers more resources than the As If of looking forward. Because future planning is familiar, you can lead your customers to a similar thinking process, which is called the conditional close.

Conditional Close

Both future planning and the conditional close have a strong component of "let's pretend." In the conditional close, you pretend you can satisfy one or more needs of your customer and ask, "So, as I understand you, if we can accomplish tasks 1, 2, and 3, then you would be glad to do business with us?" If your customer answers yes, than your job is simple.

You need to find out from your customer how s/he will know you have fulfilled all three tasks. Use the evidence procedure: what will tasks 1, 2, and 3 look like, sound like, feel like to your customer when s/he is satisfied?

Now you know what your customer wants, you have his or her outcome in sensory-based terms. If you know you can fulfill the outcome, you have a conditional close.

Let's look at an example. I am selling a communication seminar to a computer company. Small talk is over. I know my client is auditory with secondary kinesthetic, focused on the future, and concerned about communication snafus in a fast-growing company. He has the clout to sign our contract but has stopped the interaction. I assume this is because he is unsure whether my company can deliver better communication skills to his personnel.

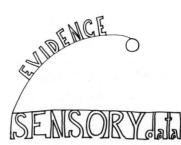

I ask, "So if we could arrange for you to talk to some of our satisfied customers, you'd feel good about signing an agreement with us?"

"Definitely. Who are your customers?"

I point to the list on our brochure, then read it aloud. He can read, but since he is auditory, hearing the names makes our customers real for him.

"American Express, Citibank, Chase Manhattan, ATEX, Sears, Tracy Lock/BBD&O, IBM."

His stern expression has relaxed a bit. "Do you have specific people I can talk to?"

Taking out my address book and writing three names and telephone numbers, I conclude, "So if they give us good marks, we can set up dates. Which month would be best for you?"

"I'll phone you within two weeks."

"Thank you for your time. I'm looking forward to working with you."

Handshake and exit.

In that exchange, I used two As Ifs: "So if we could arrange for you to talk to some of our satisfied customers, you'd feel good about signing an agreement with us?" and "So if they give us good marks, we can set up dates."

Using the conditional close early in the call saves time.

The customer went along with the first As If and balked at the second. (I do not win every round in sales. If I did, there would be no challenge.) The As If is a great time saver. You can discover within five minutes whether your product is a satisfactory match for your customer's needs. Then all you have to do is point out the match in terms your customer can understand. By educating your customer about what you have to offer to fill his or her outcome, you turn him or her into an ally.

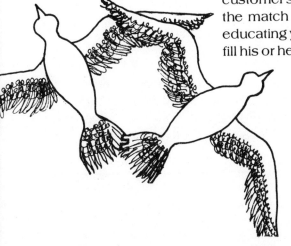

Outcome Dovetailing

Dovetailing outcomes was explained in chapter 1. The negotiation chapter (next) presents different techniques to make dovetailing a pleasure and a perfect fit. There is one technique somewhere in the book for almost every situation. If not, shake hands, move on and save time. The world is a banquet. Do not sit around a bare cupboard.

Handling Objections

The way to handle a customer's objections is to eliminate them before they arise. The elegant way to do this is to keep your customer's outcome in mind. If you are helping him to gain his outcome, and he knows this, you are not likely to hear one objection.

If he produces an objection, go back to clarifying his outcome with the ABCs of outcome setting. Objections mean that you are not accompanying the customer toward his destination. Take a deep breath, check rapport, and go for more information on his outcome.

A less effective way to deal with an objection is exaggeration. The reason this is less effective than exploring outcomes is that you can insult with exaggeration. Then the game is over.

When using exaggeration on an objection, there is a fine line between good-natured humor and insult. If you can balance on that fine line, exaggeration can be an effective tool. Exaggeration is two-edged, however, and sharp. It can cut you out of rapport and out of a sale unless done with great skill and sensitivity.

With a lot of rapport and knowing your customer, you might get away with something like this:

> *Customer:* Why should I spend the money for new tires when retreads are such a bargain?
>
> *You:* They are. And if you like that kind of bargain, you can save 100 percent by driving on the tires you have until they blow out.

However, if you are at all concerned about going too far with exaggeration as a sales response to an objective, do not try this. Go back to outcomes.

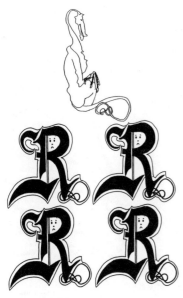

Rapport

You need rapport all the way through the sales call. Period.

Next Step and Summary

A great salesman told me once that setting up the next step at the end of the sale would prevent buyer's remorse. I do not know if this is true, but in any human transaction a summary and next step is a good idea. The next step may need a specific date—say March 15—for completion, payment, delivery, or whatever the next step is.

The stereotype of the used car salesman has tarnished a profession that renders an essential service to all of us. We are all salesmen, selling ideas, opinions, concerns and services, perhaps more often than merchandise. The processes you use to convince a friend to join you in attending a movie or to vote for a certain candidate are the same processes available to a great salesman or a hype artist. If you earn your living as a salesperson, thinking of sales in terms of processes will increase your commissions. Thinking of sales in terms of matching needs with the appropriate product will increase your credibility, confidence, and integrity.

Dovetailing prevents buyer's remorse.

Shake hands and move on.

CREATE
LOTS OF
OPTIØNS
FØR YØUR
OUTCØME

9
Negotiating with Others

Negotiation is defined here as any communication in which the *goals* of two or more parties seem to be in opposition. This broadens the picture from the formal negotiations of labor vs. management, school board vs. teachers, government vs. government. The same principles apply to *all* negotiations, whether you are deciding on a restaurant for dinner, a corporate merger, or ending a war. Again, we will be looking at process; you can supply the content.

First, decide on your outcome before you begin negotiations. It is a good idea to prepare for best-case and worst-case options as well. What would be ideal? What would you settle for? If you are part of a group, get agreement on this before negotiations with the other side begin.

You can use the same process to negotiate with your group as with the opposition. Once you and your group are clear on your outcomes, you already have an advantage. Now comes the opportunity for your skills to pay off: they will help you negotiate a settlement about which both sides feel good. The negotiation will then hold up over time, and you will not have to deal with buyer's remorse.

Second, before you begin to negotiate, get as much information as you can about the other party or parties and their positions. One area to research is any outside pressures that will affect the negotiation. These may be economic, social, political, familial, or time pressures. They affect the outcome, and the intelligent negotiator or mediator keeps these influences in mind and utilizes them from the opening stages of setting agendas to the final stage of agreeing on the next step.

Third, be sure you are negotiating with someone who can make the final decision. You do not want to make

Negotiation is any communication in which two or more parties seem to have opposing outcomes.

NEGOTIATION

your best offer and then have them retire to present your offer to someone else for a decision.

The fourth step is to get agreement that there is a basis for negotiating. Here is where fat, abstract words are useful. Maybe all you can agree on is motherhood and apple pie, or that you want both the union and the business to survive; but you must find a common, shared outcome.

Without agreement on outcomes, there is no leverage, and you might as well go home.

Never negotiate with the absent partner unless you know it and must do so

RAPPORT

OUTCOME

MAINTAIN YOUR OUTCOME
NOT YOUR POSITION

Syntonic Skills plus Tactics from Successful Negotiators

Almost all of the skills presented in this book become important in negotiation. The Pointers and the meeting format are especially useful; PEGASUS works for negotiations, just as it works for other meetings. Skilled negotiators dovetail outcomes, entertain long-term outcomes, and use summaries and questions. According to the Huthwaite Research Group report* (an excellent examination of differences between average and successful negotiators), skilled negotiators also utilize certain specific behaviors to attain their goals. Ideas from this study have been combined with key Syntonic skills in this list of recommended actions during negotiation.

- Use sensory acuity.
- Establish rapport.
- Know better than to defend and then attack (in most cases). Instead, consider the other party's proposal as one of the many options available. Remember the ABCs of outcomes. The intent behind the attack or defense, when uncovered, will give you new options

*The Behavior of Successful Negotiators. London: The Huthwaite Research Group, Ltd., 1976/78.

IN NEGOTIATION
FIRST YOU VALIDATE
YOUR OPPONENT'S
PROPOSAL

- First, validate any proposal the other side makes: "That's a very good point. If I were in your shoes, *that* would be important to me." Then restate their position, clarifying their outcome, and look for their intent.
- Seldom, if ever, use insults and irritators.
- Explicitly label questions and suggestions—for example, "Let me offer a suggestion," or "Let me ask you a question."
- Remain flexible as to sequences and options.
- Seldom, if ever, blame or accuse.
- State reasons for making a proposal, then make the proposal. This sequence is important because it cuts off potential objections. If I say I am asking for a raise, your mind immediately goes to twenty-seven reasons why you are not willing to give me a raise in pay. But if I give a legitimate reason first and then make my proposal, you are likely to attack my reason rather than my proposal.
- Give few reasons, not many. Again, the opposition will attack your weakest reason.
- Express feelings: for example, "I'm feeling concerned that . . ." Successful negotiators talk about their feelings much more than unsuccessful negotiators.

- Emphasize areas of agreement.
- Ask for time out if you need to think about some new option that has arisen.
- If you get stuck, (a) do something else; or (b) use the As If technique.
- Keep in mind that a mutual agreement comes first, but its implementation is the key to success or failure.

CHANGE REALITY

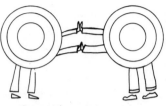

Opposing outcomes

CHANGE REALITY is a mnemonic device that is useful if the negotiation becomes blocked. The ways of thinking recalled by this acronym are sometimes called *logical levels of thought*, sometimes *abstract thinking*, and sometimes *paradigm shifts*. A *paradigm* is a map of reality plus a set of belief systems. Your paradigm limits your reality. The CHANGE REALITY techniques can remind you and your opposition of new perspectives, new views of reality, new ways to look at the things being negotiated.

Many of us get locked into thinking that only one thing will satisfy a need. Maybe this is true, but probably not. The world is full of many wondrous things, perhaps designed to satisfy somebody's needs. It is the matching of needs to satisfaction that is really tricky.

You can change the end result of the "perception plus thinking equals communication" process by changing the perceptual process or the thinking process. To match outcomes that seem to conflict, look at perception and thinking for leverage (positional advantage) for change. CHANGE REALITY techniques add choices to both perception and thinking. These thirteen tools change your way of viewing a situation so that you and the others can see options not available with your habitual responses and thought patterns.

Reality is a puzzle each of us puts together.

Chunk Up/Chunk Down

**CHUNK UP/
CHUNK DOWN
Useful for finding
the intention
behind the
demand**

Chunk is a computer term that means to break things into bits—bits of information. To *chunk up* means to move from a specific term to the general category. To *chunk down* means to move from the specific to the more specific or to component parts of the specific.

LOGICAL LEVELS   LOGICAL LEVELS OF THOUGHT

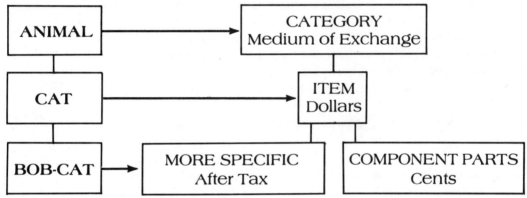

LOGICAL LEVELS

ANIMAL
CAT
BOB-CAT

CATEGORY Medium of Exchange
ITEM Dollars

| MORE SPECIFIC After Tax | COMPONENT PARTS Cents |

Say, for example, that two advertising executives are competing for one prestigious account. Their CEO grows tired of trying to decide between them and tired of their jockeying for position. He calls them in one at a time and asks two questions. The first question is, "Tell me in your own words, what does having the UNICORP account mean to you?"

Robert becomes somewhat evasive but finally, his voice full of feeling, says, "I'd know I was the top advertising executive in our firm—after you, of course. That account has always been assigned to the top man in the firm."

The CEO chunks up from prestigious account and in the category directly above writes *status.*

When Malcolm answers the same question, his words are quite different: "The CEO of UNICORP likes creative advertising. He's always been willing to take a risk in trying something new. If we keep the risks to a minimum, he'll allow us to try out new ideas no one else will be willing to underwrite. I've got some ideas. . . ." His voice trails off.

The CEO chunks up from prestigious account and in the category directly above writes *creative expression.*

The second question the CEO asks is, "If you get the account, how would your workday be different?"

Robert answers, "I'd hang the UNICORP ads from Forbes on my office walls."

Malcolm answers, "I'd be able to use Marianne's copy and see if it sells as well as I think it will."

The CEO chunks down to components of account acquisition. For Robert, he writes *Forbes ads on wall;* for Malcolm, *to check out copy effectiveness.*

The CEO then gives Robert a new title, Associate Executive Officer, which entitles him to hang copies of all the agency's ads on his office wall. Malcolm gets the UNICORP account.

In *The Art and Science of Negotiation,* Howard Raiffa uses a metaphor to describe this negotiation technique.*

CHUNK UP/ CHUNK DOWN Useful for finding out how to motivate others

*Cambridge, MA: Harvard University Press, 1982.

CHUNK UP/ CHUNK DOWN To discover new options

Raiffa calls this enlarging the pie so that everyone can have the piece they want. The thinking process of chunking up and chunking down works wonders in blocked negotiations, opening up new options. If you have a conflict and this way of thinking does not work to resolve it, do not despair. There are twelve more techniques to help everyone get what they want.

Have some fun playing with chunking up and down. Here is a list of words you can chunk. (These are not the only answers.)

CHUNK UP		CHUNK DOWN	
CATEGORY	ITEM	MORE SPECIFIC ITEM	COMPONENT PARTS
Status	Membership on board of directors	UNICORP's board of directors	Use of corporate jet, extra income, connections.
Medium of exchange	Dollars	After-tax, counterfeit, cost-of-living dollars	Cents; paper; engraving
Heavier-than-air transportation	Airplane	Piper Cub, jet, DC-7, paper	Wings, cockpit, fuselage, struts, instruments
Feeling	Anger	Deep-seated, intense, under control, emerging	Clenched hands, red face, constricted breath
Manufacturing facility	Plant	Auto-assembly plant, steel mill	Conveyor belts, lathes, furnaces

Anytime a negotiation seems deadlocked, you need to be able to chunk up and then chunk down on the disputed item. If the issue is dollars, as it often is, you may need to chunk up to the fact that dollars are simply a way of exchanging time, services, or products. In this shifting up to a broader category may lie a solution. Maybe the union wants to work a thirty-five hour instead of a forty-hour week. Its concern is not more dollars but less work time for the same dollars. Maybe they can produce the same amount of goods in less time. One option would be to go to "amount of goods produced" and trade this for dollars. Effective negotiators look for options, and chunking up and down produces them.

Hierarchy of Values and Hierarchy of Criteria

A *hierarchy* is the arrangement of items by priorities. The most important item gets a 1, the next important a 2, etc. Hierarchies of values and criteria vary with individuals and are deeply connected to the belief systems of those individuals.

Hierarchy of Values. We all have belief systems we live by. Even the worst reprobate has a bottom line, something he believes in. Maybe his belief lies in the importance of friendship; he will not welsh on a buddy. Maybe it is in his woman; he steals to buy her jewelry, and he will fight to protect her. Maybe his belief is in his country; he will enlist and die for a flag.

Our belief systems and our values are deeply connected. We are motivated and make decisions based on these belief systems and values. Often these values are unconscious. We do not know why we choose to lie or die or stay honest, but we do.

If all of us had the same values with the same priorities, things would be simple. But we do not. Some of us put a high value on the opinions of others; some do not give a hoot what others think. These people decide for themselves, regardless of others.

Not only do individuals have different values, but each person also thinks some of these values are more important than others. When one's values conflict in a given decision, the value with the highest priority will decide the outcome. If completing a report is a higher priority than being on time for an appointment, even the most punctual employee may be late for that meeting.

Knowing the opposition's hierarchy of values (i.e., which is most important, which is next, which is least important) allows you to negotiate a settlement that satisfies all sides. Even the opposition can be proud of and will live up to it, because you have respected and accommodated their value system.

The desires of human beings seem to fall into three categories, once the survival needs of food, water, shelter, and sex are satisfied. Knowing this is useful when negoti-

**CHANGE
REALITY
MNEMONIC**

C. Chunk
   up/Chunk
   down
H. Hierarchy of
   Values Criteria
A. Another
   Outcome
N. Negative
   Consequences
G. Generate a
   Metaphor
E. Enter a Counter
   Example

R. Redefine the
   Outcome
E. Effect, Cause
   and Effect
A. Apply to Self
L. Life
   Equivalents
I. Intent
T. Time
Y. Your Map of
   Reality

ating in order to know the intention behind the demand. The intention will be one of *identity*—discovering, knowing, and confirming who you are; *connectedness*—love or a feeling of belonging to a person or a group; or *potency*— a feeling that what you do has impact.

These needs seem to be natural processes that push for fulfillment. If you do not feel potent, you will be attracted to doing things to express your potency. If you do not know who you are, you will continue to test various traits, searching for the ones that are yours. Searching for congruence, perhaps. If you do not feel connected, you will search for a partner or a cause, a religion, or a group with which to feel connected.

The experts are always arguing about and trying to prioritize these needs. More important is the recognition that the priority of these needs varies from individual to individual. Then, too, needs often fall into two or three categories at once. A feeling of potency may help you know who you are. Knowing who you are may help you feel more connected. Feeling potent may reinforce your identity. These needs are connected, and sometimes one is up for satisfaction, sometimes another. Sometimes all three demand to be satisfied with one behavior.

Once you know what category it is in, you may be able to satisfy the other person's needs in many different ways. The CHANGE REALITY techniques help you find new ways of thinking to uncover these needs and then to find new options to satisfy these needs.

 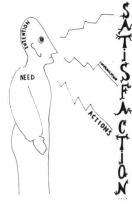

To discover your own hierarchy of values, look over this list of values, then choose six and assign numbers from one to six. One is the most important, six is the least important. These are your values and your priorities.

IDENTITY	CONNECTEDNESS	POTENCY
reputation	love	success
self-respect	my children's respect	ability to outsmart
success	family name	creativity
integrity	honor	money
my children's respect	religion	power
honesty	attractiveness	status
creativity	intelligence	talent
conventionality	admiration of others	intelligence
originality	unselfishness	independence
physical fitness	obedience	ambition
personal honor	family honor	choice
character	friendship	stubbornness
youth	ability to nurture	revenge
professional	sex	acquisitiveness
generosity	ethics	uniqueness

You may notice that many of them are related and are often the result of the three needs of identity, connectedness, and potency. These values and the beliefs around them developed from natural human needs. Be cautioned that these needs and these values and these categories will vary from individual to individual.

The way to use this hierarchy of values in negotiation is:

1. Find out the highest value of the opposition by listening to content.
2. Show them how helping you gain your outcome will satisfy their highest value or a higher value than their outcome as viewed at the time. This is a refinement of the dovetailing process. It opens new options.

Let us say you are president of a medium-sized, publicly held company. You are approached by a team of investors who want to buy all the public shares of

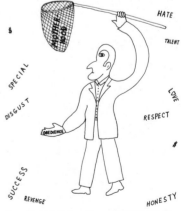

Some People's Values Seem STRANGE To Us

CREATE
LOTS OF
OPTIØNS
FØR YØUR
OUTCOME

your company at double the market value. The investors are represented by three agents authorized to make
this acquisition. The agents are willing to give you and
your staff contracts for five years to continue manag-
ing the company. You and all your stockholders will
make money.

You agree to talk the proposal over with the board of
directors. When you do, you find that neither you nor the
board wants to be acquired. You like running the publicly
held company, and the profit offered by the investment
team simply does not tempt you. You are already making enough money, and you enjoy what you are doing.
However, you really could not stop the team of investors
from buying all the stock up for sale on the New York
Stock Exchange. So rather than risk takeover, you set up
another meeting with the three agents.

About all you know about the investors is that they
want to buy a medium-sized company because (and this
is highest value) they want to make a profit. Their highest
value is profit, while you and your board value the satisfaction of running a business well. These opposed values could cause conflict.

In the meeting, you discover the potential investors
also want to diversify from their present investments,
which are in gold. Diversity would provide a safeguard
for them in a changing economy.

Your outcome is to convince them to go away and
leave you and your company alone. To do this, you look
at their highest value: money profit. An additional criterion for this profit is that it be from a different business
than gold. They also want to buy the whole company,
not a part.

In this negotiation, you utilize their highest value,
which is profit. You first point out that neither you nor
your board wants to be acquired, which causes a difficulty in itself. Then you list all the possible problems facing your company in the next five years (all true problems). And then you point out five different business
areas with greater potential for making money in the
next five years. They go away and leave you alone.

This is a simplified account of one takeover attempt I

know about. Finding the highest value of the opposition often gives you leverage in negotiating.

Another example involves a client, Irene, who is negotiating with her boss for a private office instead of a cubicle. In a shuffle of work space, she has ended up with a cubicle instead of her former office. She thought the hierarchy of values technique would be the best bet to get her outcome.

Bob and Irene are seated in his office one afternoon. Irene begins, "Bob, I've been wanting to talk to you about something I'm sure you'll be interested in knowing."

Bob replies, "What is important enough for you to make an appointment to see me? We usually handle things informally around here." Slight irritation and a note of disapproval are apparent in his voice.

"I know that, and I *like* the informality. I also like the fact that you create a business atmosphere that makes it possible for all of us to do our jobs and do them well."

"Thanks. But that's not what you came to say."

"No, you're right. That's not what I want to talk about, though it is related." She pauses.

Bob, by now quite impatient, says, "What do you want to say? Get on with it."

"It's about my new office space." As Irene says this, she can see his receptive expression change. It is now closed. Closed down. She knows Bob feels defensive about reorganizing the floor she works on. Nobody likes the new arrangement. Bob knows this but has refused to discuss the problems of the new arrangement of floor space. Irene switches tactics.

"Listen, Bob, I know you had good reason for changing the office space. I know you keep our working conditions in mind. Sometimes things don't work out exactly as planned." Bob relaxes somewhat when he hears her reflecting his own position.

He replies, "I want to leave the new arrangement for a few months and see if it doesn't work out. After

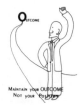

Maintain your outcome, not your position.

Emphasize areas of agreement

three months, if people are still unhappy, I'll look at the arrangement again."

Three months! Irene's heart sinks. She cannot do her best work in her assigned cubicle. Her former office had walls and a window, and she could concentrate on her work. In her new cubicle, the voices and shuffles of other people are driving her crazy.

She takes a deep breath and says, "I know you often have to make tough decisions. That's the nature of your job. You make good decisions, and people like working here. I like working here. I'm afraid my performance will fall off enough in the next three months so that you may not want *me*. I may not be able to produce the results you want." Bob had just promoted Irene, so he knows she is very capable.

"Why not?"

"Because I am constantly being interrupted and distracted by the noise around me."

"Can't you just tune out the noise?"

"Usually I can, but with these new assignments, I'm on the phone a lot. The noise is loud enough that the customers on the line are complaining about not being able to understand my words." She watches his response and knows she has him involved.

"Oh, I had no idea the noise level was that high. The customers, huh?"

Irene's office was changed the next day. The rest of the staff waited three months for their new office arrangements.

Irene knew Bob valued performance of his employees and customer good will more than his being right in a decision. She was the only worker able and or willing to utilize his hierarchy of values. When she convinced Bob her performance and customer good will were at stake, he acted to change the situation.

If Irene had told Bob she hated her new cubicle, nothing would have happened. If she had threatened to resign, he might have accepted her resigna-

WE CLUTCH OUR VALUES
TO US

tion. If she had voiced the complaints of all her co-workers, nothing would have happened. But by making him aware that his office arrangement was threatening employee performance and jeopardizing customer relations, Irene got her outcome. Other conditions were also valid and logical reasons for rearranging the office floor, but they would not have worked with Bob. He was accustomed to complaints from employees after any change in physical layout. Complaints did not move him.

Knowing someone's hierarchy of values makes it easy to present information in a way that will move that person to action. Irene had to know that being right in a decision was less important to Bob than performance and customer relations. Irene also addressed Bob's outcome when she matched her "pitch" to his values. His outcome was high employee performance and good customer relations. Moving Irene into an office ensured positive results in both areas. This is a sophisticated way to dovetail outcomes. Match your outcome to the other party's values. You both win.

How do you find out someone's top priority or his relative priorities? If you have worked with someone for a time, you probably already know his hierarchies. If he is new to you, you have to listen and ask questions. A question such as, "How did you decide to take this job?" will elicit pertinent information on values. We communicate our values with almost every sentence we speak, what we choose to talk about, and what we choose to complain about. The areas of our concerns give away our values to anyone who is tuned to listen. Our concerns are our needs. All of us have three basic needs, after survival. As we translate these needs into satisfaction, we acquire values. These values are the keys both to our actions and to changing those actions.

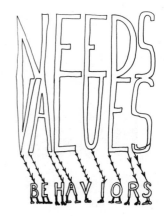

Hierarchy of Criteria. Our personal criteria are slightly different from values. Values are principles, standards, or qualities considered worthwhile or desirable. Personal criteria are those perceptions which we have judged to be important. Our personal criteria are the qualities we notice first with our five senses. We choose a certain category of external stimuli to serve as a test for what is desirable and what is not. Our criteria capture our attention and matter to us. These criteria are also called *sorting principles*: we sort through our perceptions and choose to notice those we deem important.

For example, the highest criterion for some people is other people. The most important components in their lives are people. If you ask such a person to describe the best day of his life, he will tell you about the people who were there. For others, action is their métier. In answer to the question about the best day of their lives, these people will tell you what they did. For others, where the day took place will matter, and they will give you the exact location ("on top of the Sierras"). For others, when will matter. They will give you the exact date and probably the hours involved. These are the people who remember anniversaries and do not understand how others can forget.

Our criteria are the large categories we prefer to use in sorting out the booming confusion around us. Different people have different criteria. Like a postman, each of us sorts through (or casts out into) reality for our criteria.

You can find out someone's criteria by listening and by

Some favorite criteria: people, places, time, action, information, and acquisitions.

asking simple questions. Once you know what matters to this individual, you can tailor your information to fit his or her sorting principles. You can make what you say matter by focusing on people, if people are what matter to your opposition. Let's look at an example in which two negotiators meet in James' office before the formal negotiations begin.

Facing Tim across a large desk, James begins. "I'm glad we can meet before the negotiation starts."

Tim answers, "I agree. How long have you been with ADF?"

"For several years, but I've only been conducting negotiations for them for about a year. It's quite different from what I did before."

"What did you do before?"

"I was Director of Management Performance."

"That is different. How did you happen to make the change?"

James looks thoughtful, then replies, "I was fed up with looking at all the paperwork that I had to keep track of. I wanted to work with people."

"It sounds as if you like your job now."

"I do. I've never worked with a group of people who are as cooperative. We seldom have conflicts, and when we do, we work them out until we're all satisfied. This counts a lot with me. I like a clear picture of what's going on with the people I work with. Also I see lots of expansion here, so there are opportunities for advancement."

"That's important, for sure. If you like working with people problems, you're very valuable to your company. Personnel problems are the biggest unsolved problem in business today."

Tim has already learned several important pieces of information about James. He does not know where James went to school, whether he is married, or what his salary is—and those items probably won't matter in the negotiation process. What Tim does know is that a major *sort*(important category to perceive) is people. He also knows that James likes people to cooperate in solving their problems. To have a positive impact on James and his peers,

Tim's negotiation approach will include a discussion of any decision's effect on the people involved.

Another important thing Tim learned is that James plans for the future. Some people spend a lot of time thinking about the past, some are only interested in the present moment, and some are focused on the future. The way people live in time is an important piece of information for negotiators. Tim's stated outcome will need to include future implications of the agreement.

If Tim has been watching James' eye movements and other nonverbal cues, he is probably aware of whether James prefers to trust pictures, sounds, or feelings when considering information. James' verbals indicated he is predominantly a visual, so Tim can use charts, flip-boards, and other visual aids in the formal negotiations. In five minutes of small talk, Tim has found three major keys to James' thought processes.

Another Outcome

Most people do not know what their most valued outcome is. As you probe for their outcomes, new ones often pop up—ones they did not even know they wanted, outcomes so deeply buried in their unconscious minds that they were unaware of their desires. Repeated failure to obtain outcomes conditions many people to hide their deep-seated desires. They have been disappointed so often that they protect themselves by hiding their true outcomes, even from their own conscious minds.

Be sensitive in aiding anyone to discover what s/he really wants. You may need to convince the person that it is OK for them to have the hidden outcome. You may discover s/he is maintaining *introjects*—rules, "shoulds," and "musts"—that are blocking a possible outcome.

Lucy was a stockbroker who left her secure job with an international firm to go into business with three male stockbrockers. They had picked her because she was the most successful female broker in town, and they figured she would attract the lucrative female investors in their wealthy California city. Lots of inexperienced widows were looking for sophisticated help in investing.

Lucy should have been a natural.

The new company no sooner opened than Lucy began acting in strange ways. She was forty years old and single. The first thing she did was marry an alcoholic who beat her up almost every weekend. Then she began drinking heavily herself. Her work suffered. Then she began missing work, which led to arguments with her partners. In spite of all this, her clients still poured investment money into her hands. She was attracting more investments and making more money than most of the stockbrokers in town.

The male partners decided the firm would pay for counseling for Lucy. After a couple of sessions, it was clear that Lucy had created the entire situation as the result of one rule, an introject she did not know she had. An avid feminist, she was constantly after her partners when they stepped out of line. Nevertheless, she had one residual memory that countered her conscious views on female liberation: "Women should not earn more than their male coworkers." Though her mother and father had never voiced this rule to her, they had taught her well. When her job situation changed to en-

---

Clarifying Outcomes

In discovering the other party's true outcome, keep in mind:

- *Sensory Acuity.* If the union representative lights up at your mention of a vacation in the Caribbean, maybe expense-paid vacations for employees could be traded for the disputed dollar-an-hour increase in pay.
- *Introjects.* These may block the other party from knowing its desired outcome.
- *The ABCs of Outcomes* (Chapter 1).

The inability of human beings to know what they really want and to reach out for it in a natural way is a recurrent theme in literature and poetry. This propensity is what Auntie Mame meant when she said, "Life is a banquet, and most sons-of-bitches are starving to death."

If you can help the other party sort out its most important outcome, then find a way to dovetail that outcome with yours, you will have a winning combination.

sure her earning more than her new partners, she chose all sorts of destructive behaviors so she would not violate this unconscious rule.

Once she was aware of the introject, it lost its power. Her conscious outcome of being financially successful was no longer blocked by its clever policeman , her unconscious. She stopped drinking, got a divorce, and is now the top producer in her firm.

At first sight, Lucy's outcome seemed to be failure. Her conscious outcome was blocked by an unconscious outcome, more powerful because it was unknown. Outcomes can be blocked in many different ways. Usually, outcomes are blocked by our actions, not the actions of others. Discovering our true outcomes and helping our opposition discover theirs is a powerful negotiating tool.

Negative Consequences

Many people move away from pain faster than they move toward pleasure. Certainly, all of us pull our hands from a hot stove more quickly than we sit down to a banquet. The mere threat of negative consequences is enough to persuade some people to change their outcomes. In many cases, the opposition has not considered all the things that could happen if they got their outcome. Pointing out negative possibilities can be a powerful move to induce them to look for other outcomes. Even if they obtain whatever they want in this negotiation, things will change. When things change, Pandora's Box is a real possibility. Making the possible contents of Pandora's Box explicit may cause them to rethink their original outcome.

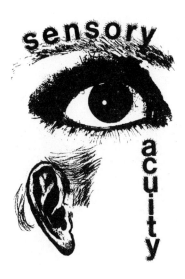

Generate a Metaphor

Metaphors are personal experiences or make-believe tales told to illustrate a particular viewpoint, make some concept clear by comparison, or lead someone's thinking toward a particular conclusion. Sophisticated metaphors are comparisons that have been disguised so that the unconscious "sees" the comparison, but the conscious mind is fooled by the disguise.

Business metaphors are best when succinct. Here are examples for two different but typical business situations:

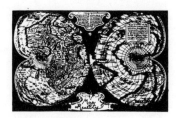

- I'm beginning to feel like a juggler with five oranges in the air, then somebody tosses me two more.
- Learning this information quickly is like trying to drink from a fire hose.

One saleswoman provided a good example of a sophisticated metaphor. Her product was a set of printed forms designed to simplify a complex legal and income tax process. The steps of the process were simple, if you followed the printed forms. She sold these forms to attorneys and accountants. When she arrived for her appointment with a potential customer, she would carefully place her car keys on the desk. Her keys had a Rubic's cube on the chain. The customer usually asked if she knew how to solve the puzzle of the Rubic's cube. She would modestly reply, "Yes." Then the buyer would ask how she learned to do it. "It was easy," she would reply, "I bought a book with all the steps laid out, one step at a time." Then she would "begin" explaining how her product could make their job easier.

Basically, a metaphor is a tale told with a purpose. The purpose in some cases, may be well-hidden, because complex metaphors are best understood by the unconscious mind, which has all five perceptual doors open all the time. This is the mind that is not bound by sequential processing, the mind that knows more than we know. This mind appreciates, is amused by, and learns from metaphors. The trick in effective communication is to line up the knowledge and energy of the unconscious with the knowledge and energy of the conscious mind. Metaphors can effect this alignment.

Comparing the familiar with the unfamiliar so that the new and strange can be added to a map of reality is a traditional use of metaphor. Another is to point out an unnoticed aspect of something familiar so we see it with new eyes. The new eyes are supplied by the metaphor's creator and carry his viewpoint. This sometimes

changes the way the listener views something already coded on his or her map. These traditional metaphors are useful in business communication if they are succinct. Greg wanted to resign his executive position and go into business for himself. He also wanted the company where he was presently employed to become a customer of his new business. Very swampy waters, right? Greg then thought back to see if he had ever experienced a similar sequence of events: moving from one position inside an organization, setting up on his own, and retaining the good will of the organization to such an extent that members of the organization were willing to bid him adieu and then pay him money for his subsequent services. The closest experience he could think of was moving away from his family and yet retaining their good will and support. He thought this breaking out of the family was an experience universal enough to be familiar to many people, including his boss.

In setting up the comparison, Greg discovered another step common to the two cases. Leaving home had been preceded by a personal change: he had turned twenty and felt mature enough to move out. Likewise, wanting to leave his firm followed a change. A recent reorganization had turned Greg's position into an unpromising spot for a young, ambitious man. Greg thought his boss realized this as well.

So Greg set up an appointment with his boss and began this way: "The last six months here at ADF remind me of a time when I was twenty years old. One day I realized something had changed. I wanted to move out from my parents' home. Things were no longer the way they had been. I felt the time had come to move out. I talked this over with my parents, got their consent, and our relationship even improved after I moved. I was grateful for what they had done for me, and they seem to be glad I was a credit to them.

"I knew I had done the right thing when they consented to come to dinner. I'm not a bad cook. I can deliver what I promise. My mother was pleased to see how much I had learned from her and was putting to good use."

Then Greg asked to discuss the way his boss viewed Greg's future at ADF. When his boss agreed that Greg's position would probably remain pretty much the same for several years, Greg said he was considering a resignation and wanted to start his own business. He told his boss his plans and said once the business was actually operating, he would like to make an appointment to discuss doing some business. Greg had total cooperation all the way.

Greg's metaphor is called a *personal metaphor*. It is very useful when you are in a ticklish situation and have a definite outcome in mind.

To design a metaphor, select one or more situations that are intrinsic to where you are and where you want to go. Then match the key components of those situations with an actual or imagined tale. (You can use heavy disguises. The unconscious is so clever that it strips away disguises with ease.) The last part of the metaphor is your outcome, disguised.

Metaphors set up strong inducements. If your outcome does not conflict with an outcome of the listener, the listener tends to unpeel the disguise and cooperate with pleasure. This pleasure is the unexpected dividend of the metaphor. Metaphors are joyous ways to influence.

Enter a Counter Example

Once our belief system has formed, we tend to delete all counter examples. If we believe the world is a dangerous place, we will continue to amass evidence to support this. If we believe the world is safe, we will sort through our perceptions for evidence of this. Whichever way we decide, we will make our answer true. This is the way generalizations work. They continue to build up evidence to support themselves, and they will delete all counter examples.

In negotiations, you may find the outcome of the opposition grows straight out of a belief system. Whether the belief system is inherited or formed by a generalization, it will be a formidable obstacle. Each brick of its foundation

Once a belief system encounters a counter example it cannot ignore, it is no longer impregnable.

represents an example the person has found to support his belief. Nonetheless, one counter example is often all that is needed to shake the belief. The edifice may not crumble, but it will certainly be easier to climb over. Belief systems have a tendency to be all or nothing.

Let me give you some examples. I have a belief that life is preferable to death. The counter example is when a person is old, ill, in pain, and wishes to die. Who am I to demand they stay alive to endure the pain?

Another belief is that killing is never the solution to a problem. The counter example is when a crazy killer has a gun at the temple of my one-year-old, and the only way to stop him is to kill him.

Here is another: I do not know what action is best for someone else. I believe that everyone knows what action is the best solution for his or her own position in life. Counter example: What if a client came to me and said that, after much deliberation, he had decided to kill himself and his family?

In negotiations as at dinner parties, avoid discussing patriotism and religion, if possible.

By producing even one counter example to the belief system supporting the opposition's outcome, you will find possible movement—leverage for a shift in position.

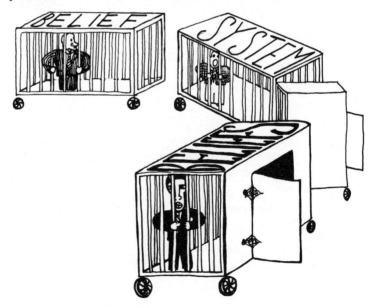

Redefine the Outcome

Language becomes your ally when you redefine an outcome. Because of the slippage between an experience and the words describing the experience, language can give you lots of leverage. If you can get the opposition to define their outcome several different times, you may find a gold mine of leverage among the definitions. You can take each word of their definition and, applying the Pointers, find out what the word means to them. Each time you can get the other side to add more words or more meanings to the definition, you have more ways to chunk up or chunk down.

Effect, Cause and Effect

Because of the stimulus-response patterns in our brains, we come to believe in a relationship between perception and experiences or between one experience and another experience. If something bad happens to me each time I see a white cat, I may decide that white cats cause bad experiences. This may or may not be true. The truth is hard to find. If I believe white cats cause bad experiences, I will make this come true. If I believe my mother always yells at me on Mondays or my boss always discriminates against me, this will probably come true.

The way to use this in negotiating is to separate cause from effect and show the opposition they are using junko logic. The main problem with cause-effect connections is that there is usually more than one cause. Cause-effect is too simple. However, it is easy to fall into this thought pattern.

Here is an example of disconnecting a cause-effect habit. Say you are negotiating with the spokesman for the Teacher's Union. You learn, from probing, that he believes teachers will do a better job if they are paid more. He wants higher salaries for the teachers so the students will benefit from better teachers.

CAUSE: Higher Salary
EFFECT: Better Teachers

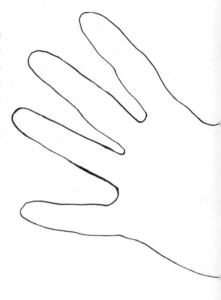

Cause—Effect and Stimulus—Response

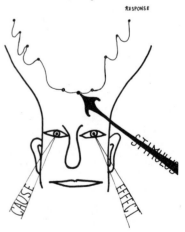

Your first move is to disconnect cause from effect. So you *cite* three documented cases in which higher salaries for teachers resulted in lower scores on achievement tests for the students. (Research literature is a fertile place to look for counter examples because we all set out to justify our reality maps, researchers included.)

A possible second move is to set up a new cause-effect theory. This sounds manipulative, and it is. Use this skill with great sensitivity while keeping the other's outcome in mind, or you will have a disaster. Junko logic is powerful, even if it is junko. We are accustomed to seeing cause-effect relationships and fall into this thought pattern easily.

CAUSE: Middle of the road salaries + scholarships for teachers for advanced degrees
EFFECT: Better teachers

You will be able to negotiate this position successfully as long as the teachers' outcome is to do a better job.

You can arrange scholarships right and left for little money, and the teachers will feel they are better prepared to do a good job. If the teachers' outcome was more money, though, this will not work. You have to find an equivalent to money to satisfy the teachers' outcome.

Apply to Self

The Apply to Self technique works for the parties in opposition and for a neutral negotiator as well. It is the old idea of stepping into someone else's shoes. The new information presented here will permit you to fit the shoes to your own feet.

The first way to do this is through rapport.

The second way is through mirroring the sensory-based data of the other. Imagine what the other person is seeing, hear what s/he is hearing, and feel what s/he is feeling. Ask the person to describe his outcome with perceptions from all three senses in sensory-based terms. While listening to these perceptions, match the person's external position and expression while imagining his internal sensations as closely as possible. You.

As if: as useful as a round table

may find extraordinary insights about his position. With your own life experiences and your new understanding of his position, you may find yourself with new resources to aid him in gaining his outcome or in finding an even better outcome for him. And for you.

The third way to use Apply to Self is to role-play the opposition for ten minutes. The opposition, of course, role-plays you. Use the role-play to state their outcome and to explore new possible solutions to any dilemmas. You may discover new routes to satisfy both sides. Then switch. The other side states your outcome and looks for new solutions. Role-playing increases understanding more than would be expected. Role-playing may turn up new options none of you had considered while your normal stimulus-response patterns were firing. Role-playing switches on a different circuit.

Life Equivalents

Finding life equivalents is a simple process. It means finding other things that yield equal satisfaction to the thing being fought over or the thing being defined. If one party has a demand the other cannot accept, substitute an alternative of equal value that both parties can accept.

The personal, individual meanings of words are based on the life experiences of the individuals, so the equivalents of any one word often vary widely among people. Each of us has different experiences, so our word meanings and our outcomes are different. Two people may be using the same word for two completely different outcomes.

Each equivalent you can dig out means another option for satisfaction, another route to the outcome. The more options exposed, the more routes explored, the better chance you have of satisfying all parties involved.

Intent

Intent was discussed at the beginning of this chapter under Hierarchy of Values. The intent behind a demand is of crucial importance in negotiating. It usually ad-

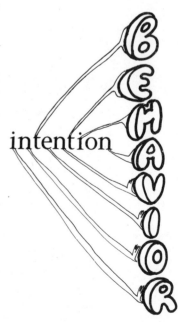

Intention pushes behavior

dresses one of these needs: identity, connectedness, or potency. If you, as negotiator, can find which category the intent falls into, then you can usually find many routes to the satisfaction of the intent.

Intent is possibly the most important unknown in negotiating. Once you uncover the other party's intent, the negotiating becomes easier. Be sure you know your own intent before you begin.

Time

Time as an External Pressure. If you know the deadline of the other party, you have an advantage. If they know you have a deadline, then they have an advantage. The clock is ticking, and this does matter to the process of negotiation.

Time as It Affects the Long-Term Outcome. Every decision has time as a component. Keeping this in mind gives you many more options, options that can accrue to your advantage in the future.

I know of a union negotiator who gladly traded his announced goal of $1.50-an-hour increase for a $.50-an-hour increase with several raises at six-month intervals. It was agreed that the $.50-an-hour was to be raised to $.65 in six months, $.75 in a year, and $1.00 in two years. He had only expected to get $.65 at the most. This long-term agreement meant that in two years he could go in for new negotiations at the $1.00 level rather than the $.65 level. He was thinking of long-range time, and the corporation negotiators were thinking of short-term savings. Considering time's effects on the outcome gives you lots of advantages.

Past-Oriented People, Present-Oriented People, and Future-Oriented People. People's perception of time and its relationship to their decision is important. Some people keep looking to the past, some are interested only in the present moment, and some are always looking to the future. In presenting information, you need to know which kind of time-orientation the other person prefers. William Faulkner depicts Southerners as past-oriented, but this may be Faulkner's own projection. If you live on a plantation whose splendor peaked in the Civil War, yes, you may look back a lot. But if your great-grandfather was a slave, and you have just graduated from law school, the present or the future will, more likely, be your elected time slot. People will tell you their time orientation with their words.

Past-oriented people are interested in the history and tradition supporting your position. Present people are interested in conditions now, and future people want to know how a negotiated outcome will affect their future situation. If the negotiated outcome will aid them in moving into a job with even better future possibilities, they will help you gain your outcome.

In Time and Through Time. One other way to use time in negotiation is to pay attention to whether the opposition lives *through* time or *in* time. In-time people remember the past so vividly that it is as if the past is the present. Through-time people bury the past so that previous experiences are not terribly important to the present moment. This goes for last year and yesterday. The way you behaved yesterday will not affect today's negotiation for through-time people. Through-time people forget yesterday and start over each morning. In-time people will remember yesterday's argument as if it just happened, and their feelings about yesterday will affect today's negotiation.

Being aware of how people process time and how they relate the negotiation process to their experience of time gives you valuable insights into how to present your information and how to structure your outcome.

Your Map of Reality

Your map of reality is what you use to make sense of the booming confusion around you. Your map is exactly right for you, no matter how crazy it looks to someone else. Given your map of reality, every decision you make and every action you take is right. All of us are making the best decisions we can at each moment.

WE
SElECT
WHAT
WE
SEE
HEAR
feel

Sometimes we look back with additional information and we wonder how we could have made such dumb decisions. However, at the time, we based those decisions on the best information available on our maps of reality. The decisions were right for us at that moment, knowing what we knew and having the experiences we had had.

If you keep this in mind, you can forgive some dumb, crazy, and impossible-to-comprehend behaviors of people around you. If you deal with people, you need this facility.

This book has given you ways to add new territories to your maps of reality. As you practice the skills presented here, your maps will become more and more complete with new information about yourself and about others. This will make your map as rich as your life. The more options in behaviors you can place on your map, the easier it will be to find and attain your outcomes. The booming confusion is rich in possible answers to your needs and intentions. Recognizing the fit of these answers to your needs becomes easier the more your awareness enriches your map.

If you enter a negotiation with an outcome that does not yet dovetail with the opposition's outcome, check your map and check their map. You may find a mutual territory of understanding or misunderstanding to explore together.

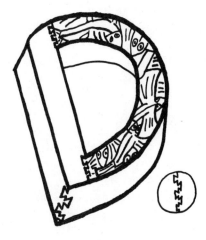

CONGRUENCE

THE TOP DOG
THE UNDERDOG
THE FATHER
THE JUDGE
THE LOVER BOY
THE MARSHMALLOW
THE MACHO MALE
THE SPORTSMAN
THE AMBITIOUS EXEC

THE YIN
THE YANG
THE SEDUCTIVE
THE MOTHER
THE WORLD TRAVELER
THE HOMEMAKER
THE NATURE LOVER
THE PURCHASING AGENT
THE BALLERINA
THE CAREER WOMAN

10 Congruence

The introduction previewed three attributes of communication excellence: sensory acuity, flexibility, and congruence. The first two were discussed in chapters 4 and 7. Now that you have learned how to develop those skills, I would like to discuss congruence, the capstone of effective communication.

Congruence comes from the Latin word, *congruens*, which means to meet together and agree. Congruence occurs when all your subpersonalities join together to work toward your outcome in a unified way. Each of us plays many roles—i.e., uses many subpersonalities—during the course of a week: business person, boss, employee, parent, bon vivant, tennis player, he-man, aesthete, and others. When our roles work in agreement, we are congruent. When they conflict, we are not.

Our behaviors and our words are often incongruent. We say one thing and do another. If we are incongruent in communication, we are less effective.

The first and most important move toward congruence is knowing our own outcomes. Because we do play many roles, and each role has its own outcome, we often need to prioritize outcomes. Once we become adept at setting outcomes, we are on our way toward congruence.

How does one achieve congruence? One way is to make sure that you really want your outcome. If parts of you are undecided about, resistant to, or uncommitted to your chosen endeavor, this incongruence will be apparent to others in your external behavior. They might notice you shaking your head no, while your words say yes. Your voice may quaver when you speak strong words. You might end a serious speech with a short giggle. All these behaviors confuse others and weaken your influence.

To feel totally congruent, spend some time role-playing your important subpersonalities. If you become aware of when you are congruent and when you are not, you may learn to appreciate your subpersonalities and their occasional opposition to each other.

Opposite tendencies inside one person are known as *polarities.* Some experts believe each of us has a polarity subpersonality for each well-developed role. In other words, if you are always a "good guy," there is a "bad boy" who is well developed and raring to get out. This bad boy can take many forms, not necessarily destructive. It may sound hard to believe, but exploring your own polarities can lead to congruence. With some exploration, you can dovetail the outcomes of your conflicting parts.

The better you know and satisfy your polarities, the more valuable you are to yourself and to your employer. The book *In Search of Excellence,* a study of forty-two successful American companies, discusses one dualism in the modern businessman: he wants to be part of a team, yet he wants to be recognized individually.* Balancing your own dualisms or polarities is possible and even profitable.

Even if you are not accustomed to thinking of subper-

* By Thomas J. Peters and Robert H. Waterman, Jr. New York: Harper & Row, 1982.

Congruence follows naturally from mastery of the syntonic techniques.

Charisma is congruence.

sonalities, you are probably aware, at times, of internal conflict. One part of your personality puts forth a position; another part opposes it or casts doubt. Internal conflicts are normal.

Some people may think subpersonalities mean you are a borderline schizophrenic. This is not true. Even the sanest have subpersonalities, whose behaviors make us interesting and effective participants in our world. Our inner conflicts are evidence of our potential flexibility.

The problem arises when some of our subpersonalities are not acquainted with others and do not know they are in conflict. The following exercise will introduce your parts to each other and allow them to work together.

INCONGRUENCE

Incongruence
cripples
communication.

Opposing parts
are the seeds
of flexibility.

Time Management and Conflict Resolution

Time is limited for all of us, and our various subpersonalities compete vigorously for it. By enlisting each part's agreement with, cooperation in, and support for each other part's need for time, we can resolve these conflicts and thus maximize the energy available for attaining our outcomes.

To demonstrate this, I have described my process for resolving inner conflict. Feel free to try this exercise for yourself, modify it to suit your particular needs, and continue using and refining it.

Say you want to schedule your time for the next month. List all the parts of your personality that want to join you in a meeting about this. Choose a time when you can be undisturbed for an hour or so (subpersonalities tend to be long-winded). Select eight parts to be invited to the meeting, and have them elect a Conflict Manager who will lead the negotiation on time allotment. Here is a list of my subpersonalities that may trigger the recognition of your own parts.

PART	COUNTERPART
Curious	Know it all
Mother	
Ambitious	Altruistic
Challenge	
Skier	
Creative	
Scuba	
Conscious	
Teacher	
Wife	Seductress
Play	
Fame-loving	Private
Comfort	Challenge
Daughter	
Love to learn	Know it all
Worker	
Friend	Loner
Conventional	Unconventional
Revenge	Forgiving
Business	Carefree
Scholar	Entrepreneur
Writer	
Painter	
Traveler	Stay at home
Humorous	Serious
Poet	
Beauty lover	
Formal	Casual
Neat	Sloppy
Organized	Disorganized, chaotic
Nesting Part	vagabond
Cook	
Pampered	Independent
Clothes horse	Blue jeans
Reader	

I looked over this list, then selected eight parts to invite to my Parts Party. The eight I invited are:

Wife
Mother
Ambitious   Altruistic
Play (ski, scuba) Work
Creative
Cook

Now I needed a Conflict Manager to handle the negotiations about time to be allotted between these eight parts. I could appoint one of them Conflict Manager, or I could create a new part on the spot to fill this role. I decided to appoint my Creative Part as Conflict Manager, because I like and trust that part. It has served me well in the past.

So we called the meeting to order. I imagined each subpersonality sitting around a boardroom table. The Cook had a white apron and chef's hat; the Creative Part was in a bright painter's smock with an artist's palette appliqued on the pocket. The Wife was in a Peck-and-Peck house dress, and the Mother was plumper than the others. The Ambitious Part wore an expensive designer suit (with boots, no less). The Altruistic Part was shirtless, having given the shirt off her back to someone. The Play Part had on a snowsuit with a scuba tank.

The party began. Immediately, the Conflict Manager (formerly Creative)

> Just desserts are
> inevitably served
> when you are not
> true to yourself.

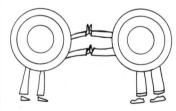

had to shout everyone down and demand that only one speak at a time. They settled down. Conflict Manager recognized the Mother. The Mother made an impassioned plea for 75 percent of my time. She concluded, "Your daughter Kathryn is young and needs a mother's care."

Conflict Manager raised the question of sleeping and waking time. Should we negotiate twenty-four hours or only the waking time, sixteen hours? In response, my Conscious Mind spoke up. She had not been invited, but she had arrived. I realized I needed her here, so I heard her out. Conscious Mind suggested we limit discussion to normal waking hours. The sleeping hours were set aside as not up for negotiation. (My Conscious Mind knows I need a lot of sleep to cope with so many strong-minded subper-sonalities.)

Not too diplomatically, Ambitious Part reminded the Mother that she had ruled over the other personalities for twenty-two years, during which time she had mothered five children. Now it was time for her to step down and allow the other members of the board to flex their muscles, so to speak.

Mother's mouth compressed, and she swelled a bit. Ambitious Part continued, saying she'd fight for 80 percent of my time. Not a bit less would do. The remaining 20 percent could be divided among the rest of the group.

The Ski and Scuba part slowly got out of her chair. The tank was heavy, and the vest on top of the padded ski jacket made her look like a beach ball. She sounded choked with emotion. "Soon I'll be too old to ski and scuba. It's now or never. I want 60 percent."

With a serious expression, the well-dressed Work Part requested the floor. The Conflict Manager, looking worried, signalled her to speak. Work Part said, "Soon I'll be too old for the marketplace as well. After forty, it's downhill in business. I'm over forty. I need 85 percent of her time."

The Conflict Manager made a swift calculation. So far, four of the nine parts had requested 300 percent of Genie's time. Conflict Manager took a deep breath, reminded herself of her Creative abilities, and heard out the next four parts. Conscious Mind said she'd carry out whatever the other parts wanted. She had no personal requests, except that Genie be conscious slightly more of the time.

The Cook wanted 30 percent, the Wife wanted 40 percent, and the Altruistic Part wanted 60 percent. Conflict Manager said she was in close contact with the Creative Part, who suggested 90 percent. So 520 percent of Genie's time would satisfy everyone. Since only 100 percent of her waking time was up for negotiation, this was an impasse.

After about fifteen minutes, a clever negotiating technique produced a resolution. Creative Part reminded the Ambitious, Work, and Altruistic parts that the writing of Genie's book would satisfy all their needs plus her own creative urges as well. Much nodding of heads. Creative Part suggested that Genie allot half her time to writing, the other half to Wife, Mother, Play, and Cook.

Some reluctance arose. "After a month we'll renegotiate," said the Conflict Manager.

The end result of the meeting:

Wife	10%	Altruistic
Mother	30%	Ambitious
Play	5%	Work
Cook	5%	Creative

(Altruistic, Ambitious, Work, Creative = 50%)

The Conscious Mind then agreed to take over the supervision of the schedule. Conflict Manager reminded Conscious Mind to be a little flexible. The meeting was adjourned.

To conduct your own conflict resolution and time allotment process: (1) make a list of major parts, (2) call a meeting, (3) set the agenda, (4) name a Conflict Manager, (5) negotiate, and (6) assign the task of supervision to the conscious part of your mind.

By using this conflict resolution process, you can get to know your parts, use the information they give you, and let them become respected internal advisors. To ensure you are behaving with maximum congruence, before you enter into a communication, make sure you know precisely what tops your list of possible outcomes. If you have prioritized your outcomes so that all your personality parts agree to work toward this particular outcome, you will be congruent in your actions, gestures, voice tones, and choice of words. Also, each of the syntonic skills will add to your congruence in communication.

Being congruent goes a long way toward satisfying your innate push for integrity. *Integrity* means being complete and undivided. Given that human beings are intrinsically whole and naturally tend toward positive (and/or pleasurable) behavior, integrity implies a soundness that can be moral or amoral, but not immoral. As the title of this book suggests, integrity is essential to the practical use of syntonics.

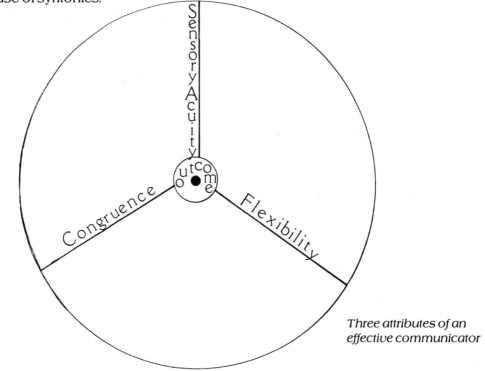

Three attributes of an effective communicator

FLEXIBILITY

Conclusion

Only you can know your own integrity: what is appropriate, just, wholesome, and valuable to you and your world. You are the authority about that. The syntonic tools do not have integrity; only human beings have integrity.

How can you keep your personal integrity and still influence people? How do you decide when to cooperate, support, or sabotage? Do you decide capriciously, or do you have a strategy that leaves you feeling good, with your integrity intact? Do you know when you have misused your influence? Even a small amount of influence contains the possibility of manipulation. (*Manipulation* is defined here as devious management for one's own advantage.) How can you avoid manipulation? When your influencing skills increase, your impact on others is stronger. Does your responsibility grow along with your power? How can you use these skills in an appropriate manner?

*Portions of this Conclusion first appeared in New Realities magazine in an article, "Playing with Power and Matches", by Bruce Dillman and Genie Laborde.

Ancient questions, yes, but the techniques for manipulation now available make thoughtful answers imperative.

If another person is involved in your outcome, the objective is to overlap that person's outcome with yours to produce a "heads I win, heads you win" situation. This is dovetailing outcomes.

Dovetailing outcomes immediately establishes rapport. Rapport is based on recognizing the humanness and needs of another person. It is entering his or her map of reality—that person's way of perceiving and coding experiences—instead of expecting him or her to navigate your map. You are able to communicate better because you are using his or her map and are more aware of the way s/he perceives and thinks. You are aware of the person's building blocks of behavior; without necessarily approving that behavior, you at least understand it.

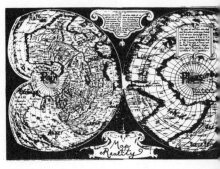

To dovetail, you need to find out the other person's outcome. Being in rapport makes this information much easier to obtain. Once in rapport, you can use the Pointers to determine his or her outcome, even if s/he is not aware of what it is. When in rapport, you are often aware of what is fair for both of you, and you are drawn toward the win-win situation—a solution in which each achieves his or her own outcome without harming the other person's interests. This is communication at its best.

Payment

A diplomat who attended one of my seminars told me that for eight years he had always negotiated hard, knowing what he wanted and usually getting it. When confronted with the concept of dovetailing, he said ruefully, "I wish I'd thought of that. My opponents often realize later they've been tricked into agreeing with my goal, and do they make me pay! All those years of paying. . . ." His expression reflected the toll of payment.

I remember another student, Bob, who is an attorney. He phoned me a month after the negotiation seminar to tell me this anecdote, which surprised him more than it did me. The idea of consciously establishing rapport with his opposition had been new to him, and he began using it every chance he could. One of his clients was suing a former employer, a large corporation. The representative of the corporation, Steve, had been meeting with Bob for some months to negotiate an out-of-court settlement. At the next meeting after the seminar, Bob had established such a deep level of rapport that Steve offered a settlement that was more than Bob's client had asked for—or deserved. The offer was so high, in fact, that Bob heard himself telling Steve to reduce his offer. Bob went on to say it would not be fair for Steve or his company, and Steve might lose his job, which was not the desired outcome. Bob knew what was fair and in keeping with the integrity of both sides in the situation.

Rapport holds up over time when one's own integrity and that of the opposition are part of the solution. Those of you who do not trust lawyers may find the above story hard to believe. Even Bob found it hard to believe; that is why he called to tell me about it.

What happens when dovetailing outcomes is not possible? There are times when the other's outcome is so abhorrent that you do not want to help him or her gain that outcome. Several options exist. One is to model your thinking processes for them (e.g., "Let me show you how I am thinking. . . ."). Once you have rapport, you can show them how you reached your own position on this. Reveal the steps of your thinking. They may like your process better than their own and stretch their map of reality to include yours.

Or they may not. Dovetailing is not always possible. If you have tried all the CHANGE REALITY techniques without finding a solution that satisfies both of you, then ending the negotiation is the next step. Or, if this is arbitration and you must reach a conclusion, adjourn for the day and begin again with the C in CHANGE (see chapter 9).

Possible solutions often go unexplored in the heat of

RAPPORT

arguing or accusation. My experience in negotiation tells me that jumping to this "let's call it quits" conclusion usually occurs long before all the possible options to dovetailing have been explored by both sides. By staying in there with these influencing techniques, we can often turn up a solution that respects both parties' integrity.

Solutions sometimes go unexplored because of power plays. People who have a slight leverage seem to need to use it. Granted power, some people need to flaunt it. The syntonic tools detailed in this book do confer personal power. Mastering these skills gives you a slight edge in most interactions. This edge increases your power to affect and influence others.

We all have the power to influence. Housewives, politicians, teachers, reporters, administrators, programmers, mothers, everyone. It is possible to have a limited amount of influence and be unaware of using skills and techniques. In most cases, this is a haphazard kind of influencing, sometimes in our direction and sometimes another. When you influence without awareness of the other person's needs and outcomes, then you are influencing in the dark. Worse yet, you may not always be conscious of crossing from influencing to manipulating.

Some people feel that as long as they use skills of influencing unintentionally, they are innocent of manipulation. This is the "innocence" of ignorance. Some of the most manipulative people I know are unaware of the techniques they use. Your awareness of syntonic techniques, though, has been anchored to the responsibility of choosing between manipulation and influencing. We cannot help but affect others. We can choose to influence positively.

When we gain skills in influencing, we increase our power to influence in the direction we want. A whole new set of concerns appears here: the concerns about personal power. If you are afraid of personal power because "they" (or you) might use it to manipulate, be aware that you do indeed have that capability. Also be aware that the syntonic tools are neutral. Only you have the choice to operate with integrity.

The syntonic tools do not have integrity; only human beings have integrity.

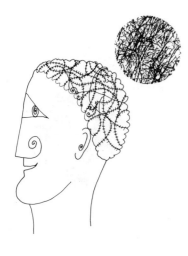

The Innocent Tool

A wise and kind woodchopper once went deep into the forest in the course of a day's work. His axe slipped, and he cut his leg deeply. He suffered much pain returning to the village but eventually recovered. While he was laid up, the townspeople, being simple folk, held a trial for the axe and found it guilty. They melted down the blade and split the handle into small pieces. Eventually, the metal was turned into bullets and the handle became matches. The woodchopper laughed when he heard about this, but he still had to buy a new axe.

Tools are neither innocent nor guilty. We use our tools in whatever way we choose. These pages have presented a formidable set of techniques: flexibility, sensory acuity, congruence, setting outcomes, rapport, Pointers, and CHANGE REALITY. Any one of these can be used to manipulate.

Where, specifically, does this danger of manipulation originate?

From them.

From whom?

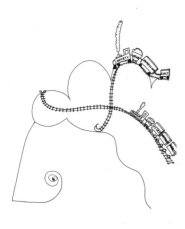

Them. Those people other than ourselves, who, because of their inherent weakness and proclivity for manipulation and skullduggery cannot be trusted with such powerful tools. You do not allow infants to play with dynamite.

In addition to the merely untrustworthy "them" are the obviously evil: criminals, subversives, corrupters, etc. What would they do with these tools? They probably would not do much they are not already doing. If they are really successful at being evil, they already have their own techniques which work very well. If by chance they are using the influencing tools, they either do it unconsciously or they already know about these techniques.

That takes care of everybody except us, and we suspect that is what a lot of the fear is about. What are we going to do with this power? Is ours an unconscious response projected onto "them" because we somehow know we are capable of evil, skullduggery, and, yes, manipulation?

Psychologist C. G. Jung wrote

> The evil that comes to light in man and that undoubtedly dwells with in him is of gigantic proportions. . . . He does not deny that terrible things have happened and still go on happening, but it is always "others" who do them. . . . This strengthens the opponent's position in the most effective way, because the projection carries the fear which we involuntarily and secretly feel for our own evil over to the other side and considerably increases the formidableness of this threat.*

* C. G. Jung, *The Undiscovered Self.* New York: New American Library, 1957.

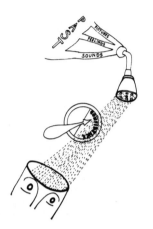

So "they" have all this power because we give it to them. Can we get it back? Jung went on to write that when we become aware of the "evil" forces within us and confront them, they lose much of their power, and we get back our power to choose.

When we choose to dovetail our outcomes with others, we are choosing personal integrity. Your outcome and the other person's may not be a perfect match, but seeking ways to dovetail avoids manipulation and protects you from resentments, recriminations, buyer's remorse, and revenge. Dovetailing is simply more practical and intelligent than manipulating.

One person told me that influencing with integrity was a contradiction in terms. Not so. We all influence. To influence well and in an appropriate way has been the concern of thinkers through the ages. Now we have superior tools for influencing. The use of these tools and the integrity of that use is in your hands.

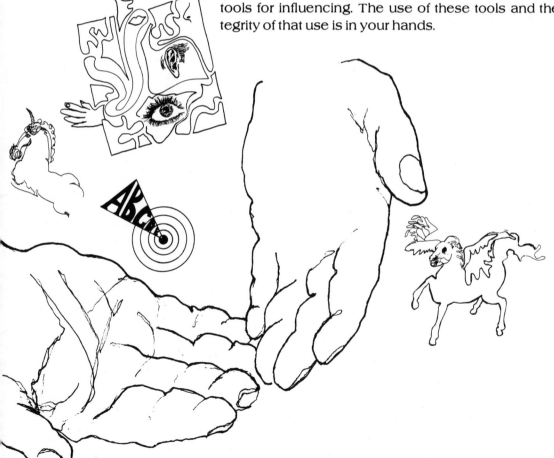

Glossary

As If technique—A way to achieve an outcome by pretending it has already happened.

Auditories—People who primarily use their ears to perceive the world and who depend on spoken words for the information that determines their behavior.

Backtrack—Review, summarize.

Calibration—Tuning oneself to recognize a certain state in another person by means of nonverbal signals.

Cerebrals—People who respond to labels (names) they give their perceptions.

CHANGE REALITY—An acronym for thirteen ways to move a blocked negotiation.

Congruence—State of being congruent.

Congruent—Unified, unimpaired, with all a person's parts working together toward his/her outcome.

Crossover mirroring—Matching the rhythm of a person's habitual movement with a different type of movement.

Dovetail—Fit together; match outcomes.

Eye accessing cues—Movements of a person's eyes in

certain directions that indicate visual, auditory, or kinesthetic thinking.

Fat (abstract) words—Nonspecific words; words with many layers of meaning.

Flexibility—Having more than one choice of behavior in a situation.

High-quality words—*see* Lean words.

In Time—Experience of remembering the past vividly.

Integrity—State of being complete, undivided, and unimpaired as well as honest.

Introjects—Unconscious rules that control behavior.

Kinesthetics—People who "feel" their way through their experiences. Kinesthetics sort both external and internal stimuli through their feelings, and they use these feelings to make their life decisions.

Lean (concrete) words—Specific words with precise or sensory-based meanings.

Low-quality words—*see* Fat words.

Map of reality—Each person's representation of the universe based on his or her individual perceptions and experiences.

Meta model—Linguistic procedures showing how the words people select limit, distort, and generalize their experiences and actions.

Metaphor—A skillfully organized story with intrinsic elements that are analogous to a present situation and also relate to a desired outcome.

Mirroring—Matching certain behaviors of someone else.

Modal operators—A linguistic term for rules ("shoulds," "can'ts," etc.).

Outcome—A specific, positive, sensory-based desired result.

Paradigm—A map of reality plus a set of belief systems.

PEGASUS—An acronym for the syntonic meeting procedures.

Perceptions—Information gathered by one or more of the senses and processed by the brain.

Pointers—Questions that lead to specific, concrete, sensory-based information.

Rapport—A process of establishing and maintaining a relationship of mutual trust and understanding between two or more parties.

Representation—Coding; storing sensory information in the brain.

Representational system—One of the five senses used for information in the brain.

Resource state—The sensory experience associated with a time when a person felt confident.

Sensory acuity—The ability to take in information by means of the senses.

Sensory-based—Relating to what a person sees, hears, feels, tastes, and smells.

Stimulus-response—An association between an experience and a subsequent so-called reaction; the natural learning process Ivan P. Pavlov demonstrated when he correlated the ringing of a bell to the secretion of saliva in dogs.

Strategy—A sequence of mental processes leading to a decision about behavior.

Through time—Experience of the past fading as time passes.

Translating—Changing predicates to indicate one representational system in lieu of another.

UNICORN—An acronym for the syntonic sales-call procedure.

Visuals—People who primarily use their eyes to perceive the world and who trust their images as a basis for decisions.

The meaning of communication
is the response you get.
If you are not getting
the response you want,
change what you are doing.

Bibliography

BUSINESS

Barnard, Chester I. *The Functions of the Executive.* Cambridge, MA: Harvard University Press, 1938; 30th Anniversary edition, 1968.

Blanchard, Kenneth and Spencer Johnson. *The One-Minute Manager.* New York: William Morrow, 1982.

Brandt, Steven C. *Entrepreneuring.* Reading, MA: Addison-Wesley, 1982.

Chandler, Alfred D., Jr. *The Visible Hand: The Managerial Revolution in American Business.* Cambridge, MA: Harvard University Press, 1977.

Cooper, Ken. *Body Business.* New York: Amacom, 1979.

Crosby, Philip B. *The Art of Getting Your Own Sweet Way.* New York: McGraw-Hill, 1982.

Deal, Terrence E. and Alan Kennedy. *Corporate Cultures.* Reading, MA: Addison-Wesley, 1982.

Drucker, Peter F. *The Changing World of the Executive.* New York: Truman Talley Books, 1982.

_____ . *Concept of the Corporation,* 2nd ed. New York: Mentor Books, 1983.

_____. *The Effective Executive.* London: Heinemann, 1967.

_____. *Management Tasks, Responsibilities, Practices.* New York: Harper and Row, 1973.

_____. *People and Performance: The Best of Peter Drucker on Management.* New York: Harper and Row, 1977.

Dyer, Willian G. *Team Building: Issues and Alternatives.* Reading, MA: Addison-Wesley, 1977.

Friedman, Milton and Rose Friedman. *Free to Choose.* New York: Avon, 1979.

Greiner, Larry and Robert O. Metzger. *Consulting to Management.* Englewood Cliffs, NJ: Prentice-Hall, 1983.

Hegarty, Christopher with Philip Goldberg. *How to Manage Your Boss.* New York: Rawson, Wade, 1980.

Helbriegel, Don and John W. Slocum, Jr. *Management,* 3rd ed. Reading, MA: Addison-Wesley, 1982.

Huseman, R.; M. Lahiff; and J. D. Hatfield. *Business Communication: Strategies and Skills.* Hinsdale, IL: Dryden Press, 1981.

Katz, D. and R. Kahn. *The Social Psychology of Organizations,* 2nd ed. New York: Wiley, 1978.

Koontz, Harold; Cyril O'Donnell; and Heinz Weihrich. *Essentials of Management.* New York: McGraw-Hill, 1974.

Levitt, Harold J.; Louis R. Pondy; and David M. Boje (eds.). *Readings in Managerial Psychology,* 3rd ed. Chicago: University of Chicago Press, 1980.

Levinson, Harry. *Executive.* Cambridge, MA: Harvard University Press, 1968.

_____. "Gut Feelings are Still the Basis for Executive Decisions," *Levinson Letter,* July 15, 1977.

Londgren, Richard E. *Communication by Objectives: A Guide to Productive and Cost-Effective Public Relations and Marketing.* Englewood Cliffs, NJ: Prentice-Hall, 1983.

Mager, Robert F. and Peter Pipe. *Analyzing Performance Problems.* Belmont, CA: Pitman Learning, 1970.

McCarthy, John J. *Why Managers Fail . . . and What to Do about It,* 2nd ed. New York: McGraw Hill, 1978.

McWilliams, Peter A. *The Personal Computer Book.* Los Angeles: Prelude Press, 1982.

Mintzberg, Henry. *The Nature of Managerial Work.* New York: Harper and Row, 1973.

Munter, Mary. *Guide to Managerial Communication.* Englewood Cliffs, NJ: Prentice-Hall, 1982.

Peters, Thomas J. and Robert H. Waterman, Jr. *In Search of Excellence: Lessons from America's Best Run Companies.* New York: Harper and Row, 1982.

Sloan, Alfred P., Jr. *My Years with General Motors.* Garden City, NY: Doubleday (Anchor Books ed.), 1972.

Williams, Frederick. *Executive Communication Power: Basic Skills for Management Success.* Englewood Cliffs, N.J.: Prentice-Hall, 1983.

EDUCATION

Averch, Harvey et al. *How Effective is Schooling? A Critical Review and Synthesis of Research Findings.* Final Report to the President's Commission on School Finance. Santa Monica, CA: The Rand Corporation, 1971.

Bandura, Albert and Robert Jerry. "Role of Symbolic Coding and Rehearsal Processes in Observational Learning," *Journal of Personality and Social Psychology,* vol. 26, no. 1, 1973.

Brown, George I. with Mark Phillips and Stewart Shapiro. *Getting It All Together: Confluent Education.* Bloomington, IN: The Phi Beta Kappa Educational Foundation, 1976.

Brown, George I. *Human Teaching for Human Learning: An Introduction to Confluent Education.* New York: Viking, 1971.

———(ed.). *The Live Classroom: Innovation through Confluent Education and Gestalt.* New York: Viking, 1975.

Cantlay, Lynne Omori. *A Study of the Relationship between Confluent Teaching and Mathematics Self-Conception in Remedial Math Students.* Doctoral dissertation, University of California at Santa Barbara, 1975.

Coleman, James et al. *Equality of Educational Opportunity.* Office of Education, U.S. Department of Health, Education and Welfare. Washington, DC: U.S. Government Printing Office, 1966.

Jencks, Christopher et al. *Inequality: A Reassessment of the Effect of Family and Schooling in America.* New York: Basic Books, 1972.

LINGUISTICS

Birdwhistell, Ray L. *Kinesics and Context: Essays on Body Motion Communication.* Philadelphia: University of Pennsylvania Press, 1970.

Hall, Edward T. *The Silent Language.* Garden City, Doubleday, 1973.

MISCELLANEOUS

Bach, Richard. *Illusion.* New York: Dell, 1977.

Castenada, Carlos. *Tales of Power.* New York: Simon and Schuster, 1974.

Grinder, John T. and S.H. Elgin. *A Guide to Transformational Grammar: History, Theory, Practice.* New York: Holt, Rinehart & Winston, 1973.

Heinlein, Robert A. *Stranger in a Strange Land.* New York: Berkeley Publishing, 1968.

Laborde, Genie Z. and Hazel Beatrous. *Tranquilizers for His Cup.* New York: Doubleday, 1961.

Machlin, Evangeline. *Speech for the Stage.* New York: Theatre Arts Books, 1980.

NEGOTIATION

Calero, Henry and Bob Oskam, *Negotiate the Deal You Want.* New York: Dodd, Mead, 1983.

Fisher, Roger and William Ury. *Getting to Yes.* Boston: Houghton Mifflin, 1981.

Huthwaite Research Group Limited. *The Behavior of Successful Negotiators.* London: 1976/78.

Nierenberg, Gerard I. *Fundamentals of Negotiating.* New York: Hawthorn Books, 1973.

Raiffa, Howard. *The Art and Science of Negotiation.* Cambridge, MA: Harvard University Press, 1982.

NEUROLINGUISTICS

Bailey, Rodger. "Neurolinguistics: Information Processing in the Human Biocomputer." *J.C. Penney Forum,* November 1982.

Bandler, Richard and John Grinder. *Frogs into Princes.* Moab, UT: Real People Press, 1979.

_____ . *Patterns of the Hypnotic Techniques of Milton H. Erickson, M.D.,* vol. 1. Cupertino, CA: Meta Publications, 1976.

_____ . *Reframing.* Moab, UT: Real People Press, 1982.

_____ . *The Structure of Magic,* vols. 1 and 2. Palo Alto: Science and Behavior Books, 1975 and 1976.

Bandler, Richard; John Grinder; and Virginia Satir. *Changing with Families.* Palo Alto: Science and Behavior Books, 1976.

Cameron-Bandler, Leslie. *They Lived Happily Ever After.* Cupertino, CA: Meta Publications, 1978.

Dilts, Robert. "Let NLP Work for You," *Real Estate Today.* February 1982.

Dilts, Robert; Leslie Cameron-Bandler; Richard Bandler; John Grinder; and Judith DeLozier. *Neuro-Linguistic Programming, vol. 1.* Cupertino, CA: Meta Publications, 1980.

Farrelly, Frank and Jeff Brandsma. *Provocative Therapy.* Cupertino, CA: Meta Publications, 1978.

Goleman, Daniel. "People Who Read People," *Psychology Today.* July 1979.

Gordon, David. *Therapeutic Metaphors.* Cupertino, CA: Meta Publications, 1978.

Gordon, David and Maribeth Meyers-Anderson. *Phoenix: Therapeutic Techniques of Milton H. Erickson, M.D.* Cupertino, CA: Meta Publications, 1981.

Grinder, John and Richard Bandler. *The Structure of Magic, vol. 2.* Palo Alto: Science and Behavior Books, 1976.

———. *Trance-Formations.* Moab, UT: Real People Press, 1981.

Laborde, Genie Z. "Don't Eat the Menu," *New Realities,* vol. IV, no. 1. December, 1981.

———. "Neuro-linguistic Programming," *New Realities,* vol. IV, no. 1. April, 1981.

Laborde, Genie Z. and Bruce Dillman. "Playing with Power and Matches," *New Realities,* vol. IV, no. 4. December, 1981.

Lankton, Steve. *Practical Magic.* Cupertino, CA: Meta Publications, 1979.

Maron, Davida. "Neurolinguistic Programming: The Answer to Change?" *Training and Development Journal.* October 1979.

Moine, Donald J. *A Psycholinguistic Study of the Patterns of Persuasion Used by Successful Salespeople.* Dissertation 1981 study, University of Oregon. Ann Arbor, MI: University Microfilms International, 1982.

Zientara, Marguerite. "IBMer Tells How to Handle a Primadonna," *Computerworld.* November 15, 1982.

PHILOSOPHY

Buber, Martin. *The Way of Man.* Secaucas, NJ: Citadel, 1973.

Fromm, Erich. *The Art of Loving.* New York: Harper and Row, 1956.

Fuller, Buckminster. *I Seem to Be a Verb.* New York: Bantam, 1970.

Kaufman, Walter. *Existentialism from Dostoevsky to Sartre.* Cleveland, OH: World, 1956.

Sartre, Jean-Paul. *Being and Nothingness.* New York: Philosophical Library, 1956.

PSYCHOBIOLOGY

Eccles, J.C. *Facing Reality.* New York: Springer Verlag, 1970.

Lashley, K.S. *The Neuropsychology of Lashley.* New York: McGraw-Hill, 1960.

PSYCHOLOGY

Assagioli, Roberto. *Psychosynthesis.* New York: Viking, 1971.

Auerswald, Edgar. "Thinking About Thinking About Mental Health," *American Handbook of Psychiatry*, vol. II, 2nd ed.; ed. Gerald Caplans. New York: Basic Books, 1974.

Barron, Frank. *The Shaping of Personality: Conflict, Choice and Growth.* New York: Harper and Row, 1979.

Baumgardner, Patricia. *Legacy from Fritz.* Palo Alto: Science and Behavior Books, 1975.

Bentov, Itzhak. *Stalking the Wild Pendulum: On the Mechanics of Consciousness.* New York: Bantam Books, 1977.

Berelson, Bernard and Gary Steiner. *Human Behavior: An Inventory of Scientific Findings.* New York: Harcourt Brace and World, 1964.

Bialer, I. "Conceptualization of Success and Failure in Mentally Retarded and Normal Children," *Journal of Personality,* vol. 29 (1961).

Brown, Judith R. *Back to the Beanstalk.* La Jolla, CA: Psychology and Consulting Associates Press, 1979.

Crandall, V.C.; W. Katkovsky; and V.J. Crandall. "Children's Belief in Their Control of Reinforcement in Intellectual-Academic Achievement Situations," *Child Development,* vol. 36 (1965).

Dement, William. *Some Must Watch While Some Must Sleep.* San Francisco: W.H. Freeman, 1972.

Downing, Jack. *Gestalt Awareness: Papers from the San Francisco Gestalt Institute.* New York: Harper and Row, 1976.

Downing, Jack and Robert Marmorstein (eds.) *Dreams and Nightmares.* New York: Harper and Row, 1973.

Enright, John. *Enlightening Gestalt: Waking Up from the Nightmare.* Mill Valley, CA: Pro Telos, 1980.

Fagan, Joen and Irma Shepherd (eds.). *Gestalt Therapy Now.* New York: Harper Colophon Books, 1970.

Freud, Sigmund. *Beyond the Pleasure Principle.* London: The International Psycho-Analytical Press, 1922.

_____ . *Civilization and Its Discontents.* London: The Hogarth Press and the Institute of Psycho-Analysis, 1973.

_____ . *The Ego and the Id.* London: The Hogarth Press, Ltd., 1957.

_____ . *The Future of an Illusion.* Garden City, NY: Anchor Books, 1957.

_____ . *Group Psychology and the Analysis of the Ego.* New York: Liveright Publishing Corporation, 1951.

_____ . *Moses and Monotheism.* New York: Vintage Books, 1939.

_____ . *New Introductory Lectures on Psycho-Analysis.* London: The Hogarth Press, 1974.

_____ . *On the Interpretation of Dreams.* London: George Allen and Unwin, Ltd. 1954.

_____ . *An Outline of Psycho-Analysis.* New York: W.W. Norton, 1949.

_____ . *The Question of Lay Analysis.* London: Imago Publishing Company, Ltd., 1947.

_____ . *Totem and Taboo.* New York: Vintage Books, 1946.

Gaines, Jack. *Fritz Perls Here and Now.* Millbrae, CA: Celestial Arts, 1979.

Hampden-Turner, Charles. *Maps of the Mind.* New York: Macmillan, 1981.

Huxley, Laura Archera. *You Are Not the Target.* North Hollywood, CA: Wilshire Book Co., 1972.

Janov, Arthur. *The Primal Scream.* New York: Dell, 1971.

Jones, Ernest. *Papers on Psycho-Analysis.* London: Bailliere, Tindall and Cox, 1950.

Jung, C. G. *Man and His Symbols.* New York: Dell, 1964.

_____ . *Modern Man in Search of a Soul.* New York: Harcourt, Brace & World, 1933.

_____ . *The Portable Jung.* New York: Penguin, 1976.

_____ . *Psyche and Symbol.* Garden City, NY: Anchor Books/Doubleday, 1958.

_____ . *The Undiscovered Self.* New York: New American Library, 1957.

Klein, Melanie; P. Hermann; and R. E. Money-Kyrle (eds.). *New Horizons in Psycho-Analysis.* New York: Basic Books, 1955.

Laborde, Genie Z. "Comparing Certain Theories and Therapies of Freud and Perls," *The Gestalt Journal,* Spring 1979.

_____ . *An Exploration into the Practicability of Using Confluent Approaches in Increasing Awareness of Introjects.* Doctoral dissertation, University of California at Santa Barbara.

Laborde, Genie Z. and George I. Brown. "Introjects and Their Relationship to Locus of Control," *Integrative Therapie,* January 1981.

Laing, R.D. *The Divided Self.* New York: Pantheon Books, 1969.

_____ . *The Politics of Experience.* New York: Balantine Books, 1968.

_____ . *Self and Others.* New York: Penguin Books, 1972.

Laing, R.D. and A. Esterson. *Sanity, Madness and the Family.* New York: Penguin Books, 1970.

Lawrence, D.H. *Psychoanalysis and the Unconscious: Fantasia of the Unconscious.* New York: Viking, 1921.

Lichtenstein, E. and W. Craine. "The Importance of Subjective Evaluation of Reinforcement in Verbal Conditioning," *Journal of Experimental Research in Personality,* vol. 3, 1969.

Lilly, John C. *Programming and Metaprogramming in the Human Biocomputer.* New York: Bantam, 1972.

Maslow, Abraham. *Toward a Psychology of Being.* New York: Van Nostrand Reinhold, 1968.

McClain, E. W. and H. B. Andrews. "Self-Actualization among Extremely Superior Students," *Journal of College Student Personnel,* 1972.

Meissner, W. W. "Notes on Identification III: The Concept of Identification," *Psycho-Analytic Quarterly,* vol. 41, 1972.

Menninger, Karl. *A Psychiatrist's World.* New York: Knopf, 1937.

_____. *The Human Mind.* New York: Knopf, 1937.

Milgrim, Stanley. "Behavioral Study of Obedience," *Journal of Abnormal and Social Psychology,* vol. 67, no. 4, 1963.

_____. "Some Conditions of Obedience and Disobedience to Authority," *Human Relations,* vol. 18, 1965.

Moustakas, Clark E. *Loneliness and Love.* Englewood Cliffs, NJ: Prentice Hall, 1972.

Ornstein, Robert E. (ed.). *The Nature of Human Consciousness.* New York: Viking, 1974.

Perls, Frederick. *Ego, Hunger, and Aggression.* New York: Vintage Books, 1967.

_____. *The Gestalt Approach and Eye-Witness to Therapy.* Palo Alto: Science and Behavior Books, 1973.

_____. *Gestalt Therapy Verbatim.* Toronto: Bantam, 1971.

_____. *In and Out of the Garbage Pail.* Toronto: Bantam 1972.

Piaget, Jean. *The Psychology of Intelligence.* London: Routledge and Kegan Paul, Ltd., 1950.

Polster, Erving and Miriam Polster. *Gestalt Therapy Integrated.* New York: Vintage Books, 1973.

Shepard, Martin. *Fritz: An Intimate Portrait of Fritz Perls and Gestalt Therapy.* New York: E. P. Dutton, 1975.

Stafford-Clark, David. *What Freud Really Said.* New York: Schocken Books, 1971.

Stoller, Frederick H. *Encounter.* San Francisco: Jossey Bass, 1970.

Wolman, Benjamin (ed.). *The Handbook of Clinical Psychology.* New York: McGraw-Hill, 1965.

Wilber, Ken. *The Spectrum of Consciousness.* Wheaton, IL: Theosophical Publishing, 1977.

SOCIOLOGY

Berger, Peter and Thomas Luckmann. *The Social Construction of Reality.* New York: Grove Press, 1966.

Campbell, Joseph. *The Hero with a Thousand Faces.* Princeton, NJ: Princeton University Press, 1972.

Gottesfield, H. and G. Dozier. "Changes in Feelings of Powerlessness in a Community Action Program," *Psychological Reports,* vol. 24, no. 1, 1963.

Hampden-Turner, Charles. *Radical Man: The Process of Psycho-Social Development.* Garden City, NY: Anchor Books, 1971.

Hollingshead, A. B. *Elmstown's Youth: The Impact of Social Classes on Adolescents.* New York: Wiley, 1949.

Kahl, Joseph. *The American Class Structure.* New York: Rinehart and Company, 1953.

Katz, I. "The Socialization of Academic Motivation in Minority Group Children," *Nebraska Symposium on Motivation,* ed. D. Levine. Lincoln: University of Nebraska Press, 1967.

Kohn, Melvin. *Class and Conformity.* Homewood, IL: The Dorsey Press, 1969.

Kuhn, Thomas S. *The Structure of Scientific Revolution.* Chicago: University of Chicago Press, 1962.

Leonard, George. *The Transformation.* New York: Delacorte, 1972.

Liebow, Elliot. *Talley's Corner.* Boston: Little, Brown, 1967.

McLuhan, Marshall and Quentin Fiore. *The Medium Is the Message.* New York: Random House, 1967.

Meadows, Donelia et al. *The Limits of Growth.* New York: Universe Books, 1972.

Pearce, Joseph Chilton. *Exploring the Crack in the Cosmic Egg.* New York: The Julian Press, 1974.

Thompson, William I. *At the Edge of History.* New York: Harper and Row, 1972.

Wilber, Ken. *Up from Eden.* Garden City, NY: Anchor Press/Doubleday, 1981.

SYSTEMS THEORY

Bertalanffy, Ludwig Von. *Robots, Men, and Minds: Psychology in the Modern World.* New York: George Braziller, 1967.

Maltz, Maxwell. *Psycho-Cybernetics.* New York: Pocket Books, 1969.

Satir, Virginia. *Peoplemaking.* Palo Alto: Science and Behavior Books, 1972.

Index

A
A B C's of outcomes   8, 113, 172
Aggressive behavior, how to soften   24
Agreement on outcomes, gaining   118
Apply to Self technique   179-180
Arbitration   197
As If technique   146, 149, 180
Auditory mode   53
 internal/external   56
 characteristics of   54, 62

B
Bandler, Richard   90, 127
Behavior, as part of communication process   113
 flexibility in   129, 131
 habitual   133
 identity with   133-135
Belief systems   162
Body postures, matching   35, 63
 changes in   78
Brain, function of   45-47
Brainstorming, in meetings   125
Breathing   15, 53, 61
 matching   33, 38
 changes in   78, 81
 and representational systems   60-64
Business meetings (See meetings)   111-126
Buyer's remorse   153

C

Calibration   81
Cause and effect, disconnecting   178-179
Cerebral mode, characteristics of 65
CHANGE REALITY   158, 173, 197
Changes, interpreting   77
Choices, increasing of   136, 158
Chomsky, Noam   90, 127
Chunk up/chunk down   159-161
Coding (See Maps of reality)   47, 50, 53, 68
Communication   45, 75
  process of   69, 89
  content of   89
  role of behavior in   129-130
  as feedback system   131
  flexibility in   129-130
Comparators   105-108
Competence, trust in   29, 30, 36
Conditional close, in sales   148
Congruence   3, 118, 126, 185
Connectedness (See Needs, human)   163-164
Conscious thought processes   56
Context, influence on perception of   55, 56, 67, 114
Counter examples, use in negotiations   176
Credibility, gaining   29, 37, 144
Criteria (See Hierarchy of criteria)   162-171
Crossover mirroring   34

D

Dovetailing of outcomes   20, 21, 22, 87, 106, 150,
   155, 164, 186, 196, 201
Deletion   43, 47
Distortion   43, 47

E

Enlarging the pie   161
Evidence, as criteria for successful meetings   117
Eye movements   58-73
   visual   58, 60
   auditory   62
   kinesthetic   64
   cerebral   65
   pictures   59, 61
   photographs   76A

F

Fantasy, use of in sales   146
Fat and lean words   12
Feedback   20, 24, 43
Feedback systems (See communication)   131
Flexibility   3, 129-139
   in setting outcomes   139
   blocks to   132, 135
   disadvantages of   135-136
   advantages of   136-137
   practice of   137

gaining of   137-139
in outcomes   139
Future planning (see As If technique)   146
best case/worst case   153

G
Generalizations   43, 47, 101-104
Goals   7, 10, 16
Grinder, John   90, 101, 127
Group communications   (See Meetings)   111
Gustatory   56

H
Hidden agendas   118, 121
Hierarchy of criteria   162-168
Hierarchy of values   162, 169-171

I
Identity (see Needs, human)   163-164
Incongruence   15, 118, 185-187
Influencing positively   198
Integrity   192, 195, 197
Intention (See Needs, human)   131, 163, 180
Introjects (See Rules)   98-101, 172
Intuition   52, 75

K

Kinesthetic mode   11, 53
  internal/external   56
  characteristics of   54, 64
Korzybski, Alfred   48, 90

L

Language systems, individual   108
  slippage   49
Life equivalents   180
Lower lip, changes in   78, 80
  photographs   76H

M

Manipulation   21, 59, 196, 199
Maps of reality   47-50, 68, 158, 162-163, 196
  expansion of   158-175, 183
Matching   144
  voice   31
  breathing   33
  movement   34
  body postures   35
  representational systems   30-36
Meaning, as response/behavior   131
Meetings   111-126
  goal of   111
  syntonic procedures for Pegasus   111-126
  environment of   114

two-thirds rule for   113
    establishing rapport in   113
    take over of   124
Memory, accessing   143
Meta Model, the   90-101
Metaphors, use of in negotiations   173
    personal   176
Mirroring   30, 34-36, 144, 179
    crossover   34
Minute muscle changes   78, 80
    photographs   76B, 76G
Miscommunications   130
Model operators (See rules)   98-101
Movement rhythms, matching   34

N
Needs, human   163, 168
Negative consequences, use of in Negotiations
        173
Negotiation   153-183
    outcomes in   153-154, 183
    best-case/worst-case options   153
    blocked   158-173
    tactics   156-157
Next step, in sales   151
Nouns, unspecified   92

O

Objections, handling in sales   150
Olfactory   56
Optimum state (See Resource state)   15, 115,
    142-143
Outcomes   3, 5, 7-24, 48, 113, 153, 186, 192
  ABCs of   8, 113, 172
  specifying   8, 16, 19
  dovetailing of   20-22, 87, 106, 150, 155, 158, 164,
      186, 196, 201
  long- and short-term   23
  using Pointers to obtain   106
  presenting at meetings   116-118
  flexibility in setting   132, 139
  blocked   132
  checking w/ sensory-based data   172
  customer's, in sales   141
  hidden   171
  disguised in metaphors   176
  redefinition of   178
  dealing with unacceptable   197
  positive   11, 15, 16

P

Pacing and leading   144
Paradigm shifts   158
Parts   118, 186-191
PEGASUS meeting procedures   111-126

Perception   45, 47, 51
  doors of (See Representational systems)   51
Pointers, the   89-108, 113, 132, 196
  use in sales calls   145
Polarity responses   28, 133, 186, 188-191
Potency (See Needs, human)   163-164
Power plays   198
Priorities (See Hierarchy of Values)   164

Q
Qualifying the buyer   144

R
Rs, the four   21, 142, 145, 201
Rapport   22, 27-38, 196, 197
  ascertaining   27, 36
  establishing   24, 28, 30, 33, 34, 113
  breaking   38
  in meetings   113, 116, 121
  in sales   151
  in negotiations   179
  maintaining   36
  photographs   76A
Relevancy challenge, in meetings   120
Remorse, Recrimination, Resentment, and Revenge
      (See Rs, the four)   21, 142, 145, 201
Representational systems   53-73, 113
  and eye movements   58-73

visual   53, 54, 60
auditory   53, 64
kinesthetic   53, 64
matching of   68-73
categories   55
words   70-71
photographs   76A
Resource states   15, 142, 143
Role playing   186, 188-191
Rules, as limitations   98-101

S
Sales techniques (See Syntonic sales techniques)
    141-151
See/feel/hear/questions (See Sensory based data)
    20, 139
technique   146
Sensory acuity   75-87, 131, 132
    training of   76, 77
    benefits of   24, 87
    use in meetings   118
    as guide to behavior change   38
Sensory-based data   9, 23
    positive nature of   11
    use in determining success of
        meetings   113, 117
    checking outcomes with   8, 11, 139
    use in creating resource states   139

use of in sales   143, 146, 148
  mirroring of others   179
Sub-personalities   187, 188-189
Skin color, changes in   78, 79
  photographs   76C, 76D, 76E, 76F
Smell, sense of   54
Sorting principles (See Hierarchy of criteria)   169
Stimulus-response, use of   143
Structure of Magic, The   90
Summarization   119
  of major decisions in meetings   119
  of next step in meetings   122
  in sales   151
Syntonic learning   91
Syntonic meeting procedures (See PEGASUS)
    111-126
Syntonic model   2, 126
Syntonic sales techniques   141-151

T
Taste, sense of   54
Thinking, process of   43, 45, 68
Time
  personal perceptions of   181-182
  use of in negotiations   171, 181
Trust   36
  establishing   28, 30, 37
Two-thirds rule, the   113

U

Unconscious, the   51, 52, 55
Unconscious, visible responses   28
UNICORN   145

V

Values (See Hierarchy of Values)   162-171
Verbs, unspecified   97-98
Visual mode,   53
    internal/external   56
    characterstics of   54, 60
Voice
    matching of   30, 33
    incongruence in   15

W

Words   47
    fat and lean   12
    as symbols for experience   47, 49
    as content of communication   89
    Sensory-based   23
    choice of   53
    and representational systems   60, 62, 70, 71

Genie Z. Laborde's newest medium is video. She has recently completed a video training package that increases the understanding and retention of the skills presented in her seminars. The seminar training focuses on the next level of the skills presented here in *Influencing with Integrity*.

Produced by professionals in a documentary format, the twelve modules of video show more than one hundred business men and women in communication interactions that typify those of a working day. The training video uses the basic concepts of accelerated learning. The music for the video was composed especially for the series by Steven Halpern.

The twelve modules are:

PERCEPTION IN COMMUNICATION
VISIBLE SIGNS OF
INVISIBLE PROCESSES
OUTCOMES
MAPS OF REALITY
SENSORY AWARENESS
RAPPORT
SYNERGY OF SIX
SUPER QUESTIONS
STIMULUS RESPONSE
STATE OF EXCELLENCE
METAPHOR
DOVETAILING

The video package was audience tested at Pacific Bell during production then purchased by Pacific Bell upon completion. Chase Manhattan Bank purchased the package eleven days later and IBM soon after. After reviewing the film, Jake Bius, Sr. Educator at IBM, concluded, "Absolutely the best training video I've ever seen . . . gets to the meat of interpersonal relationships in business."

For more information, phone 800/228-4069 Outside California
415/326-5613 In California
212/938-8957 In New York
Or write: Grinder Laborde Associates 1433 Webster St.
Palo Alto, CA 94301

PERSONAL NOTES